A SHORT HISTORY

OF

THE BRITISH IN INDIA

A SHORT HISTORY

OF

THE BRITISH IN INDIA

ARTHUR D. INNES

GYAN

Published by

GYAN

Gyan Publishing House
5, Ansari Road
Daryaganj, New Delhi-110002
Phone: 011-47034999, 9811692060
E-mail: books@gyanbooks.com

Distribution Network
gyanbooks.com
India, USA, Canada, UK, Australia

ISBN: 978-93-6780-037-9 (PB)

First Published, 1919

2nd Impression 2024

Printed at: Gyan Press, Delhi.

A SHORT HISTORY OF THE BRITISH IN INDIA
Author: ARTHUR D. INNES

THE BRITISH IN INDIA

A SHORT HISTORY
OF
THE BRITISH IN INDIA

BY

ARTHUR D. INNES

SOMETIME SCHOLAR OF ORIEL COLLEGE, OXFORD

WITH EIGHT MAPS

SECOND EDITION

METHUEN & CO. LTD.
36 ESSEX STREET W.C.
LONDON

TO THE READER

THE object of the present volume is to set before the ordinary reader the story of the steps by which India came gradually to be painted red on the map—of the development of the British Supremacy out of the Tenancy of a Trading company; a development fostered by the best brains and watered by the best blood of Britain. I have attempted to do this within the compass of a single volume of a size and form which can be handled with ease: and to do it as fully as the space permits, accurately, clearly, and (I hope) not unattractively. The author's objects.

For the serious student of Indian History, such a volume can only be made the basis for further study; but it should help him to get a preliminary grip of the whole subject which will be of material assistance in classifying and in co-ordinating the detailed information which must be derived from other sources. That a book is wanted which will serve that purpose I infer from the fact that in spite of a fairly extensive acquaintance with the literature of the subject, I have never succeeded in finding one. Sir Alfred Lyall has indeed gone near to supply it in his "British Dominion in India," but from the time of Lord Wellesley, his narrative lacks the fulness of the earlier chapters. On the other hand, such a work as Marshman's is too bulky for the purpose—at least, it is more than four times the length of this volume.

Macaulay's Essays have made Clive and Warren Hastings more or less familiar to most of us; but the period of progress from Warren Hastings to the Mutiny is to most minds very nearly a blank. It seems tolerably obvious that having on our hands the responsibility for governing India, we ought not to leave the study of Indian conditions—which involves the study of Indian History—entirely to candidates for the Indian Civil Service, while reserving the right to comment on their subsequent administration on the strength of data derived either from our own inner consciousness or from newspaper articles which have been called into being for the purpose of advocating a particular course at a moment of crisis.

Authorities. In an appendix to this volume, I have given with details a list of books which may with advantage be consulted in dealing with particular persons, periods, and episodes—a list which might of itself be expanded into a volume. That list as it stands comprises: (1) Official records: (2) Standard Historical works: (3) Detailed Biographies: (4) Essays on aspects of the subject: (5) Studies at first or second hand of episodes or persons. For the *verification* of facts, the first class is obviously the most important; it is from the second and the last that we must ordinarily, for the most part fill in the outlines; from the third and fourth that we must obtain detailed specific knowledge. Here however, I may mention that *Marshman's History* is the most satisfactory general account with which I am acquainted, as Elphinstone's remains the standard account of the Hindu and Mohammedan periods. The entire series of the "*Rulers of India*," issued by the Clarendon Press, is admirably adapted for intelligent popular consumption, though suffering from the inevitable defect that each writer is disposed more or less consciously to become the advocate of his particular subject. And Sir Alfred Lyall's "*Asiatic Studies*"—may one, in such a connection mention also his *Verses written in India*?—and Sleeman's *Rambles and Recollections* are the most illuminating studies of the Oriental mind.

Spelling. I would add here some remarks on the rule I have followed in spelling Indian names. As late as thirty years ago it was the custom to anglicise the spelling of every word. Recently a Scientific method has been adopted; Macaulay's *Budge-budge* has become Báj Báj; and the Map-makers give us Machlipatnam for Masulipatam. On the other hand, while studying the period of the Sikh wars, I noted at least six different ways of spelling Firozshah; and even under the orthodox editorship of Sir William Hunter it has been found impossible to maintain an absolutely uniform spelling.

Again, there is one respect in which the modern orthodox spelling is trying: that is in the use of the accent to distinguish between long and short vowels. To read of the "Rájá" has a peculiarly irritating effect, something like reading a page peppered with words in italics, nor is it in any way helpful to have Allháhábád thrust upon you: these symbols often render no aid towards discovering the syllable on which stress is laid. I have therefore generally dispensed with accents in the text, but on the first occurrence of a name and in the glossary I have introduced the long and short marks ¯ ˘ where it seemed likely that the reader would thereby be helped to a more correct pronunciation.

There are certain words and names which may fairly be regarded as having passed into English Literature. Such are Arcot and Plassey, Assaye, Lucknow, Cawnpore, the Mogul, rupee, sepoy. To discard these forms is very much like writing of Aelfred and Eadward. Wherever such a form appears to me to be really established, I have kept to it. Where two forms are almost equally familiar, as with Haidar Ali and Hyder Ali, I have adopted the more modern one, mentioning the alternative where the name comes in for the first time. Where usage has not established any particular form, I have endeavoured to conform to the system of the "Imperial Gazetteer" save for the omission of accents. Roughly speaking, to find the common equivalent of the old quasi-phonetic spelling in the modern form, and *vice versâ*, the following tables may be useful:—

TABLE OF TRANSLITERATION

Showing the commoner variations found in the Modern spelling.

Old	Modern	Old	Modern
ai	e	M*ai*r	M*e*r
au	a	Punj*au*b	Panj*a*b
aw	a	ad*aw*lut	ad*a*lat
e	i	F*e*rozepore	F*i*rozpur
ee	i	M*ee*rut	M*i*rat

Old	Modern	Old	Modern
oa	o	Br*oa*ch	Bar*o*ch
oo	u	Hind*oo*	Hind*u*
ou }	{ ao	ch*ou*t	ch*au*th
ow }	{ au	Morari R*ow*	Morari R*ao*
ore	ur	Nagp*ore*	Nagp*ur*
"	ar	Chundernagore	Chandarnag*ar*
u	a	Meer*u*t	Mir*a*t
y	ai	Kh*y*ber	Kh*ai*bar
c hard	k	*C*abul	*K*abul
c soft	s	*C*ircars	*S*arkars
g soft	j	*G*ingee	*J*in*j*i
x	ks	Bu*x*ar	Ba*ks*ar

e mute in the old spelling is omitted in the modern: *e.g.* Feroz*e*pore becomes Firozpur.

Values of Letters in Modern Spelling

As commonly pronounced by the British in India.

ā : as a in *call* or *palm*.	ă : as a in *man* or u in *up*.
ē : as a in *mate* or *hare*.	ĕ : as e in *men*.
ī : as i in *police*.	ĭ : as i in *fit*.
ō : as o in *pope*.	ŏ : as o in *hot*.
ū : as oo in *pool*, *poor*.	ŭ : as u in *put*.
ai : as i in *site*.	ao, au : as ow in *owl*.

ch, ph, sh, th, j, w, and y all follow the ordinary English pronunciation: but p-h and t-h are sometimes sounded separately. n is sometimes nasal (Fr. *bon*), *e.g.* in Bhonsla.

ANALYTICAL CONTENTS

BOOK I.—HINDU AND MOHAMMEDAN DOMINATION

CHAPTER I

THE LAND AND THE PEOPLE

CHAPTER II

MOHAMMEDAN DOMINION

CHAPTER III

THE MOGUL DISRUPTION, AND THE MARATHAS

§ 2. ORGANISATION

CHAPTER XVII

THE SYSTEM

CHAPTER XVIII

LAND SETTLEMENT

CHAPTER XIX

GENERAL PROGRESS

BOOK IV.—THE COMPLETION OF BRITISH DOMINION

PAGE

CHAPTER XX

TRANS-INDUS: A RETROSPECT

CHAPTER XXI

THE AFGHAN EXPEDITION: AUCKLAND AND ELLENBOROUGH

CHAPTER XXII

SINDH AND GWALIOR: AUCKLAND AND ELLENBOROUGH

BOOK V.—THE CONFIRMATION OF SOVEREIGNTY

PAGE

CHAPTER XXVII

THE EVE OF THE MUTINY

CHAPTER XXVIII

REVOLT

CHAPTER XXIX

CONQUEST AND GENERAL CONSIDERATIONS

CHAPTER XXX

EPILOGUE

MAPS

CHRONOLOGICAL SUMMARY

Leading events are printed in heavy type.

Events outside the Indian radius are printed in italics.

The name of each Governor-General is printed in small capitals, at the time of his entering on the office.

The chapters in which events are narrated are denoted in the left hand column.

§ *I. From the first Mohammedan Invasion to the commencement of the Anglo-French struggle.* [*Book I.*]

(*i.*) *Pre-Mogul period.*

II.	664	First Mohammedan (Arab) invasion.
	1001-1026	Mahmud of Ghazni.
	1176-1206	Shahab-ud-Din (Mohammed Ghori).
	1189	*Richard I. of England.*
	1206-1288	Slave Dynasty of Delhi.
	1215	*The Great Charter.*
	1272	*Edward I. of England.*
	1288-1321	Khilji Dynasty of Delhi.
	1314	*Bannockburn.*
	1321-1412	Tughlak Dynasty of Delhi.
	1346	*Crecy.*
	1347	Bahmani Dynasty in the Dekhan.
	1398	Tamerlane's Invasion.
	1414-1450	Seiad Dynasty of Delhi.
	1415	*Agincourt.*
	1450-1526	Lodi Dynasty of Delhi.
	1453	*Constantinople taken by the Ottoman Turks.*
	1489	The Five Kingdoms of the Dekhan.
	1498	**Vasco di Gama rounds the Cape and reaches Kalikat.**
		Nanuk, founder of the Sikh sect, *fl.*
	1507	Albuquerque at Goa.
	1517	*Luther and Tetzel.*

(*ii.*) *Mogul Period.*

II. 1526 **Baber's Conquest of Hindostan.**

1531 Humayun succeeds Baber.

1533 *Henry VIII.'s Reformation Parliament.*

1540 Humayun expelled. Sher Shah.

1555 Humayun restored.

1556 **Akbar** succeeds Humayun.

1558 *Queen Elizabeth.*

1588 *Defeat of the Armada. Naval supremacy passes to England.*

IV. 1600 **English East India Company.**

1601 *Dutch East India Company.*

II. 1605 **Jehangir** succeeds Akbar.

IV. 1613 British Factory established at Surat.

1615 Sir T. Roe's Embassy to the Mogul.

1620 First British settlement in Bengal.

II. 1627 **Shah Jehan** succeeds Jehangir. Sivaji born.

IV. 1632 Overthrow of Portuguese power in Indian seas.

1639 First British settlement at Madras.

1653 *Cromwell's* charter to the E.I.C.

II. 1658 **Aurangzib** deposes Shah Jehan.

III. 1659 **Sivaji** in the Dekhan.

IV. 1660 *Charles II.*

1661 *Death of Mazarin.*

1662 Acquisition of Bombay from Portugal.

1664 **French E.I.C. constituted.**

1666 *France and Holland in Alliance.*

1668 *England and Holland in Alliance.*

1670 *France and England in Alliance.*

1672 *War between England and Holland.*

1674 *Peace with Holland.*

1678 *Secret treaty between Charles II. and Louis XIV.*

III. 1679 Aurangzib attacks Bijapur.

1680 Death of Sivaji.

1685 War between British and Aurangzib.

1686 Fall of Bijapur.

1687 Fall of Golconda.

1688 *William of Orange becomes King of England*

IV. 1690 Establishment of Fort-William (Calcutta).

1698 Rival English East India Company.

III., XX. 1700 Govind Singh (Sikh Guru) *fl.*

IV. 1701 **François Martin.**

1702 Amalgamation of E.I. Companies.

III. 1707 **Death of Aurangzib.** Bahadur Shah Mogul.

(*iii.*) *The Mogul Disintegration.*

III. 1712 Jehandar Shah Mogul.
1713 *Treaty of Utrecht.*
Farokshir Mogul.
1714 *Accession of House of Hanover.*
1715 *Death of Louis XIV.*
1717 Balaji Wiswanath Peshwa.
1718 Puppet Moguls, under the Seiads.
1719 Mohammed Shah Mogul.
1720 Baji Rao I. Peshwa.
IV. 1721 Lenoir Governor at Pondichery.
III. 1724 Asaf Jah (Nizam ul Mulk) established in Dekhan.
1733 *Bourbon Family Compact.*
IV. 1734 Dumas Governor at Pondichery.
III. 1737 Extension of Maratha Ascendancy in Hindostan.
1739 *War declared between England and Spain.*
Nadir Shah sacks Delhi.
IV. 1740 Dumas resists the Nagpur Raja.
III. Balaji Rao Peshwa.
Anwar-ud-Din Nawab of Carnatic.
Sadat Khan Nawab Wazir of Oudh.
Ali Vardi Khan Nawab of Bengal.
IV. 1741 **Dupleix Governor of Pondichery.**
VI. 1744 *War declared in the West between France and Great Britain.*
1745 Rise of the Rohillas.
The Nawab of Arcot protects the French.
1746 *Jacobitism extinguished at Culloden.*

§ *II. Rise of the British Power.*

(*i.*) *Anglo-French Contest in the Carnatic.*

1746 Commencement of the contest in the Carnatic.
La Bourdonnais captures Madras (Sept.).
Dupleix retains Madras. French troops defeat the Nawab's army.
1747 Unsuccessful attacks on Fort St David.
Appearance of Griffin's squadron.
1748 Stringer Lawrence holds Fort St David (June).
Unsuccessful siege of Pondichery.

VI. 1748 *Peace of Aix-la-chapelle.* **Restoration of Conquests.**
Death of Nizam-ul-Mulk. Disputed succession.
1749 Dupleix ransoms Chanda Sahib.
Anwar-ud-Din killed at Ambur.
Departure of British Fleet.
Mohammed Ali at Trichinopoli.
Muzaffar Jang Nizam (Dec.).
1750 Muzaffar Jang killed; Salabat Jang Nizam.
1751 The Nizam withdraws to Haidarabad with Bussy.
Robert Clive: Capture and defence of Arcot.
1752 French surrender at Trichinopoli. Death of Chanda Sahib.
1753 Northern Sarkars granted to Bussy by Nizam.
1754 **Dupleix recalled.**

(ii.) *The Company becomes a Territorial Power.*

VII. 1756 Suppression of the pirate Angria by Clive and Watson.
Black Hole of Calcutta (July).
The Seven Years' War begins.
Clive and Watson enter the Hugli (Dec.).
1757 Clive in Calcutta (Jan.).
Capture of Chandernagar (March).
The Omichund treaties (May).
Battle of Plassey (June).
Clive supreme in Bengal. Mir Jafar Nawab.
Pitt's great administration begins (June).
VI. 1758 Madras: arrival of Lally (April).
Lally captures Fort St David.
Bussy summoned to the Carnatic from Haidarabad.
Madras besieged (Dec.).
Development of Pitt's Naval Policy.
1759 Siege of Madras raised (Feb.).
Forde captures Masulipatam (April). Northern Sarkars ceded to British.
VII. Shah Alam's futile invasion of Bengal.
Collision with the Dutch on the Hugli.
Victories of Quebec and Quiberon.
VI. 1760 **Victory of Wandewash** (Jan.).
Clive leaves India (Feb.).

VI. 1760 *Accession of George III.* (Oct.).
1761 Capture of Pondichery. End of French power in India.
VIII. **Ahmed Shah Durani overthrows the Marathas at Panipat.** Madhava Rao Sindhia escapes. Death of Balaji Rao Peshwa.
Siege of Patna raised by Calliaud and Knox.
1762 **Haidar Ali seizes the throne of Mysore.**
Mir Cassim made Nawab of Bengal.
1763 *Peace of Paris.*
Massacre of Patna, and flight of Mir Cassim.
1764 *Grenville's Stamp Act.*
Battle of Buxar: Munro overthrows the Nawab-Wazir of Oudh.
1765 **Clive returns to India**, to "cleanse the Augean Stable."
The Nawab Wazir confirmed in the throne of Oudh.
The Mogul grants the Diwani of Bengal, and the Northern Sarkars, to the Company.
1766 Clive's reforms. The Double Batta incident.
Rockingham Ministry (July).
1767 Clive leaves India.
Grafton Ministry (July).
1768 Madras treaty with Nizam.
1769 Madras treaty with Haidar Ali.
1770 *Lord North's Ministry.*
IX. 1771 Shah Alam Mogul, under Maratha protection.
1772 Disputed succession at Puna.
Warren Hastings Governor of Bengal.
The Company resolves to "stand forth as Diwan."

(iii.) *The Rule of Warren Hastings.*

IX., XVII. 1773 **North's Regulating Acts.** Warren Hastings appointed Governor-General.
IX. **Suppression of the Rohillas.**
1774 Nana Farnavis at Puna.
WARREN HASTINGS Governor-General. The New Council and Judges.
Clive commits suicide.
The Calcutta Triumvirate over-rule Hastings.
1775 Asaf-ud-daulah succeeds as Nawab-Wazir (Oudh).
Bombay treaty of Surat with Ragoba (March).
X. Calcutta Council supports Nuncomar against Hastings.

X.	1775	Hastings' letter of Resignation.
		Beginning of American War of Independence.
		Execution of Nuncomar.
IX.	1776	Treaty of Purandar with Marathas.
		Lord Pigot, Governor of Madras, deposed.
		Monson (one of the Triumvirate) dies.
	1777	The Chevalier St Lubin at Puna.
X.		Contest as to Hastings' resignation. Death of Clavering. **Hastings predominant.**
		Burgoyne's surrender at Saratoga.
	1778	*France openly supports America.*
		Death of Chatham.
IX.		Hastings authorises a Maratha war.
		Seizure of French ports.
	1779	Disaster of Wargam.
		Goddard's march across Hindostan to Surat.
		Nizam's scheme for Anti-British confederacy.
X.		Contest between the High Court and Council (Calcutta).
		Spain joins France against Britain.
IX.	1780	Goddard in Gujerat.
X.		Impey made head of the Sadr Adalat.
IX.		**Haidar Ali invades the Carnatic.** Baillie's disaster.
		Gwalior captured by Popham.
		Eyre Coote sent to Madras (Nov.).
	1781	Holkar checks Goddard.
		Sindhia defeated in Malwa.
		Coote's victories in the Carnatic.
		Negapatam captured. Braithwaite's disaster.
X.		**Benares insurrection.**
		Surrender of Yorktown.
IX.	1782	Suffren's battles with Hughes.
		Rodney's victory of the Saints. Naval predominance recovered.
		Shelburne ministry (July).
X.		**Affair of the Oudh Begums.**
IX.		Treaty of Salbai with Marathas.
		Death of Haidar Ali : Tippu Sahib Sultan.
	1783	Operations at Gudalur. *Treaty of Versailles.*
		Fullerton in Mysore.
		Coalition Ministry (April). Fox's India Bill (Dec.).
	1784	Treaty of Mangalur with Tippu.
		Pitt with Dundas in power.
XI., XVII.		**The Pitt-Dundas India Act.**
X.	1785	Hastings leaves India.

§ *III. Development of British Ascendancy.*

(*i.*) *Cornwallis and Shore.*

XI.	1785	SIR JOHN MACPHERSON *ad interim.*
		Sindhia's claim for tribute to the Mogul repudiated.
	1786	Tippu at war with the Nizam and Puna.
		CORNWALLIS (Sept.).
		Arrangements made in Oudh.
XVII.	1787	Administrative reforms of Cornwallis.
	1788	*Impeachment of Warren Hastings.*
		Declaratory Act on Indian Government.
XI.		The Nizam and the Guntur Sarkars.
	1789	Letter of Cornwallis to the Nizam.
		Fall of the Bastille.
		Tippu attacks Travancore.
	1790	Campaign of Medows against Tippu.
	1791	Cornwallis's first campaign against Tippu. He captures Bangalur, but has to retreat.
	1792	Cornwallis's final campaign. Tippu submits.
		Acquisition of Mysore districts.
XVIII.		Beginning of Ryotwari land settlement in Madras presidency.
		The "September Massacres."
	1793	*Beginning of the great French War.*
		Permanent zemindari settlement in Bengal.
XVII.		Company's Charter Act.
XI.		SIR JOHN SHORE, afterwards Lord Teignmouth.
	1794	Death of Madhava Rao Sindhia (Mahdoji). He is succeeded by Daulat Rao.
	1795	French influence at Haidarabad. Raymond's corps.
		Cape of Good Hope taken.
		Mutiny of Bengal officers.
	1796	Shore concedes the military demands.
		Baji Rao II. Peshwa.
		Bonaparte in Italy.
	1797	New treaty with Oudh.
		Mornington appointed to succeed Shore.
		Battles of Cape St Vincent and Camperdown.

(*ii.*) *Wellesley.*

XII.	1798	LORD MORNINGTON, afterwards MARQUESS WELLESLEY.

Chapter	Year	Event
XII.	1798	Wellesley reaches Calcutta (May).
		Alarm of Afghan invasion under Zeman Shah.
		The Mauritius Proclamation made known (June).
		Fresh alliance with the Nizam.
		Battle of the Nile (*Aug.*).
	1799	**Conquest of Mysore.** Death of Tippu (May).
		Re-establishment of Hindu Dynasty in Mysore.
		Partition of Mysore.
		Carnatic, Surat, and Tangier under British rule.
	1800	*Battle of Marengo.*
		Malcolm's Embassy to Persia.
		"Subsidiary" cessions of territory by the Nizam.
XVIII.		Munro engaged on *Ryotwari* Settlement: Madras.
XII.		Egyptian expedition under Baird.
		Death of Nana Farnavis. Rise of Jeswant Rao Holkar and Amir Khan, and of Ranjit Singh.
		Wellesley foiled in his plan to seize the Mauritius.
	1801	New treaty with Oudh: Henry Wellesley. **Oudh territories ceded.**
		Pitt resigns.
		Battles of Alexandria and Copenhagen.
		Rise of the Barakzais in Afghanistan.
		Peace of Amiens.
		Wellesley's resignation declined.
[illegible]	1802	Holkar defeats Sindhia and the Peshwa before Puna.
		Baji Rao surrenders Maratha independence by the **Treaty of Bassein**
	1803	*War with France renewed.*
		Coalition of Marathas. **Maratha War** (Aug.). Victories of **Assaye** (Sept.), **Laswari** (Oct.), **Argaon** (Nov.).
		Treaties with Sindhia and Bhonsla.
	1804	*Napoleon made Emperor. Pitt takes office again.*
		Holkar renews the Maratha war. Monson's disaster.
		Ochterlony's defence of Delhi. Battle of Dig.
	1805	Failure of Lake at Bhartpur.
		Wellesley retires.

(*iii.*) *Non-Intervention.*

Chapter	Year	Event
XIV.	1805	CORNWALLIS (July). He dies in Oct.
		SIR GEORGE BARLOW (Oct.) *ad interim.*
		Lake's pursuit of Holkar. Terms made with Sindhia.
		Fall of Dundas. Battle of Trafalgar (Oct.).
		Death of Pitt. Ministry of "All the Talents" (Jan.).

XIV. 1806 Terms made with Holkar.
Vellur mutiny. Bentinck recalled from Madras.
Battle of Jena.
1807 *Treaty of Tilsit.*
LORD MINTO.
1808 *Peninsula War begins. Growing coolness between Tsar and Napoleon. Convention of Cintra.*
Persian Missions of Harford, Jones, and Malcolm.
Missions to Kabul, Panjab, and Sindh.
1809 Barlow at Madras: collision with Madras officers.
Percival Prime Minister. Battles of Corunna, Talavera, and Wagram.
Treaty with Ranjit Singh. Protectorate of Cis-Satlej.
Minto supports Nagpur against Amir Khan.
1810 *Torres Vedras.*
Capture of Mauritius.
XX. Afghanistan; expulsion of Shah Shuja; the Barakzais.
1811 *Albuera.*
XIV. Seizure of Java.
Rise of the Pindaris.
1812 *Lord Liverpool Prime Minister.*
Napoleon's Russian Expedition.
Minto superseded.

(*iv.*) *Renewed Expansion.*

1813 *Battles of Vittoria, Dresden and Leipzig.*
XVII. Renewal of E.I.C. charter.
XV. LORD MOIRA, afterwards LORD HASTINGS
Ghurka aggression.
1814 **Ghurka War.** Early disasters.
Aggression of Pindaris in Central India.
Hastings supports Bhopal against Marathas
Persian treaty.
1815 Success of Ochterlony against the Ghurkas.
Treaty with Nepal.
Intrigues of Baji Rao Peshwa.
European War ended by Waterloo.
1816 Hastings resolves to suppress Pindaris. George Canning's dispatch.
Subsidiary alliance accepted for Nagpur by Apa Sahib.
1817 Hastings extends alliances and prepares Pindari campaign.

XV. 1817 **War begins** (Pindari and Maratha) Oct.
Battles of Kirki and Sitabaldi (Nov.).
Suppression of Pindaris and Pathans.
1818 Subjection of Central India. Sattara state set up.
Surrender and deposition of Baji Rao. **Maratha treaties. Annexation of Maratha territory.**
Panjab: Ranjit Singh takes Multan.
1819 The Nawab of Oudh made king.
Death of Warren Hastings.
Ranjit Singh annexes Kashmir.
XVIII. 1820 Elphinstone and the Bombay Land Settlement.
XV. The affairs of Palmer & Co.
XIX. 1821 Captain Hall in Merwara.
XV. 1822 Lord Hastings resigns.
Suicide of Castlereagh; prevents Canning from assuming the office of Governor-General.
XVI. 1823 LORD AMHERST.
Burmese challenge to war.
1824 **Burma war declared** (Feb.).
Barrackpore mutiny.
Rangoon taken.
1825 Difficulties of the troops in Burma.
Occupation of Prome.
Outram among the Bhils.
The Bhartpur troubles.
1826 Fall of Bhartpur (Jan.).
Successes in Burma.
Peace: **cession of Assam, Arakan, and Tenasserim.**
XX. Dost Mohammed supreme at Kabul.
Russo-Persian war.

(*v.*) *An Interval of Rest.*

1827 **Russo-Persian rapprochement.**
1828 *Wellington Prime Minister.*
LORD WILLIAM BENTINCK.
XIX. 1829 Movement to check Infanticide.
Decree abolishing Suttee.
1830 *Lord Grey Prime Minister.*
Sleeman's campaign against Thuggee.
XX. 1831 Mission of Alexander Burnes to Sindh and Lahore.
1832 *Reform Act.*
XVI. Annexation of Kurg and Kachar.
Administration of Mysore taken over.

XVII.	1833	**Revised Charter Act.**
		Death of Daulat Rao Sindhia.
XVIII.		Robert M. Bird in the North-West Provinces.
	1834	Increased control over Rajput princes.
XXV.		Director's dispatch, discouraging adoption.
XIX.		The education problem acute.
	1835	**Educational victory of the Western School.**
XVI.		SIR CHARLES METCALFE *ad interim.*
		Liberation of the Press.
XIX.		Dixon in Merwara.
XXI.	1836	LORD AUCKLAND.
	1837	*Accession of Queen Victoria.*
XX.		Persian advance on Herat.
		Peshawar finally secured by Ranjit Singh.
		Mission of Burnes to Kabul.
		Siege of Herat begun (Nov.).

§ *IV. Completion of British Dominion.*

(*i.*) *Auckland, Ellenborough and Hardinge.*

XXI.	1838	Auckland resolves to restore Shah Shuja.
		Siege of Herat raised.
		Preparations for Afghan Expedition.
	1839	British advance from Shikarpur (Feb.).
		Kandahar occupied (April). Ghazni captured (July).
		Death of Ranjit Singh (June).
		Restoration of Shah Shuja at Kabul (Aug.).
	1840	Surrender of Dost Mohammed.
		Macnaghten and Burnes at Kabul. with British army.
	1841	Rising at Kabul. Murder of Burnes and Macnaghten (Dec.).
	1842	**Kabul Disaster** (Jan.).
		Defence of Kandahar and Jellalabad,
		LORD ELLENBOROUGH (Feb.).
		Retirement ordered. Siege of Jellalabad raised (April).
		Nott and Pollock instructed to withdraw *via* Kabul (July).
		Kabul re-occupied (Sept.).
		Triumphal withdrawal from Afghanistan.
		Charles Napier in Sindh.
		Restoration of Dost Mohammed.
XXVI.		Macpherson among the Khonds.
		P. and O. Company instituted.

XXII.	1843	Battle of Miani (Feb.). **Sindh annexed.**
		Gwalior: death of Jankoji Sindhia (Feb.).
		Maharajpur campaign (Dec.).
		Panjab: murder of Maharaja Sher Singh.
XIX.		Thomason in the North-West Provinces.
XXII.	1844	New arrangements at Gwalior.
		Mutinies of Sepoys ordered to Sindh.
XXIII.		Recall of Lord Ellenborough.
		SIR HENRY afterwards LORD HARDINGE.
		Domination of the Khalsa in the Panjab.
	1845	Ganges Canal.
		Sikhs cross the Satlej (Dec. 11).
		Battles of Mudki (Dec. 18) and Firozshah (Dec. 21 and 22).
	1846	Battles of Aliwal (Jan. 26) and **Sobraon** (Jan. 10).
		Lahore treaty (March). Cession of Jalandar and Kashmir. Sale of Kashmir to Gholab Singh.
		Bhairowal treaty (Dec.).
		Repeal of Corn Laws.
	1847	Henry Lawrence in the Panjab to end of year.

(ii.) *Dalhousie.*

	1848	LORD DALHOUSIE (Jan.).
XXIV.		Revolt of Mulraj at Multan (April).
		Herbert Edwardes before Multan (July).
		Sher Singh raises the Khalsa (Sept.).
		Gough enters the Panjab (Nov.).
		Battles of Ramnagar (Nov.) and Sadulapur (Dec.).
	1849	Battle of Chillianwalla (Jan. 13).
		Fall of Multan (Jan. 22).
		Battle of Gujerat (Feb. 21).
		Panjab annexed (March 30).
		Governing Board established in Panjab.
XXV.		**Annexation of Sattara.** Adoption Annexation.
XXIV.	1851	Troubles with the Burmese Government.
	1852	Ultimatum to Burma.
		Capture of Rangoon (April 11).
		Capture of Prome (Oct.).
		Annexation of Lower Burma.
		John Lawrence chief commissioner of Panjab.
		Aberdeen Ministry.
XXV.	1853	Annexation of Jhansi.
		Annexation of Nagpur.

XXV.	1853	Assignment of Berar by the Nizam.		
		Claims of the Arcot family, and of Nana Sahib as heir to Baji Rao, rejected.		
		Renewal of Charter.		
XXVI.		Railway construction.		
		Cheap postage.		
	1854	Sir Charles Wood's Education dispatch.		
		Crimean War begins.		
	1855	Electric telegraph.		
		Palmerston Premier.		
		Fall of Sebastopol.		
	1856	End of Crimean War.		
XXV.		**Annexation of Oudh** (Feb.).		

(iii.) The final stage.

XXVII.	1856	LORD CANNING (Feb.).		
		General Service Enlistment Act.		
		Disturbances in Oudh.		
		Persian War.		
	1857	Jan.		**Cartridge incident.**
				Sporadic mutinies.
				Treaty with Dost Mohammed.
				China War.
		May	10	**Mirat outbreak.**
			11	Mogul proclaimed.
XXVIII.			28	Series of mutinies begins.
		June	6	Allahabad secured.
			12	**Ridge at Delhi occupied by British.**
			14	Gwalior Mutiny.
			26	**Fall of Cawnpore.**
			30	Havelock takes command at Allahabad.
			30	**Siege of Lucknow Residency begins.**
		July	17	**Havelock reaches Cawnpore** after hard fighting.
			29	Havelock crosses Ganges into Oudh.
		Aug.	12	**Havelock falls back to Cawnpore.**
				Oudh clansmen join the Lucknow mutineers.
		Sept.	6	Siege train reaches Delhi.
	1857	Sept.	14	**Storming of Delhi walls.**
			15	Outram's junction with Havelock.
			21	Delhi cleared of mutineers.
			25	**Outram and Havelock enter Lucknow.**
XXIX.		Nov.	12	**Sir Colin Campbell relieves Lucknow.**
	1858	Mar.		Capture of Lucknow by Sir Colin Campbell.

XXIX.	1858	April	Capture of Jhansi by Sir Hugh Rose.
			Canning's Oudh proclamation. Recrudescence of the war in Oudh.
		Dec.	**End of the war.**
XXX.			Transfer of Government of India to the Crown.
			End of the H.E.I.C. Lord Canning first Viceroy.

A SHORT HISTORY

OF THE

BRITISH IN INDIA

BOOK I

HINDU AND MOHAMMEDAN DOMINATION

CHAPTER I

THE LAND AND THE PEOPLE

(*Maps I. and II.*)

THE great territory to which we give the name of India is separated from the rest of Asia by a vast bulwark of tremendous mountains, forming a kind of arc round its northern half, the ends of the arc resting on the sea. One half of her frontier is the mountains, the other half is the ocean. Outside the barrier lie Biluchistan and Afghanistan, Turkistan, Tibet, Burma. On one side only, the western, does the great barrier offer practicable passes. Therefore it is either through the Suleiman mountains by one of those gateways, or by crossing the sea, that the stranger has always made his way into India. The Himalayan chain from Kashmir to Assam has been an impassable wall. **Boundaries.**

From North to South, parallel to the Suleiman range, and along its base, flows the great river Indus; joined by the united waters of five great streams. The land through which those rivers flow is the "Land of the Five Rivers," the Panjab or Punjaub. Below the junction is Sindh. East of Sindh, east and south of the Panjab, is a great expanse of territory having but little water, and in part sheer desert, named Rajpŭtāna or Rajasthan. **Hindostan.**

Only a little east of the Sătlej (Sutledge), the most easterly of the Panjab rivers, the Ganges and the Jămna (Jumna) take their rise in the Himalayas, flowing at first almost due south, then sweeping eastward to mingle at Allahabad, and thence onward in the same direction till the sacred stream takes a sudden turn south to empty its waters into the Bay of Bengal. Other great rivers join it on its way, the country through which they pass being described generally as the Ganges basin. From the mountains of Assam and Tibet on the far East the mighty Brahmapūtra descends to join the Ganges almost where it reaches the sea. The lower portion of the Ganges basin is Bengal; the name of Hindostan is sometimes restricted to the upper portion.

Carrying the eye southward down the map; the mountain chain of the Vindhyas runs inland from the western coast, extending to Orissa on the east: the river Nerbadda (Nerbudda), flowing from East to West, skirting its southern foothills. The Nerbadda is the southern boundary of Hindostan in the larger sense of the term; the line being continued to the East coast, corresponding approximately to the course of the Mahanadi (Mahanuddy). Thus applied, the name of Hindostan covers the Northern half of India, as that of Dekhan or Deccan covers the southern half.

The Dekhan. South of the Nerbudda, along the west side of the peninsula, separated from the sea by only a narrow strip of plain, the Western Ghāts rise steeply; forming the western side of a plateau which falls slowly towards the east, from which side it is comparatively, but only comparatively, easy of access. The stretch of plain between the hills and the coast is much wider on the east than on the west. The course of the great rivers Godaveri and Krishna shows the fall of the country. The fundamental distinction to be observed is, that Hindostan is in the first place richer and therefore more tempting to the invader than the Dekhan, and in the second place that it is more easy of access. The Vindhyas form a barrier between the Dekhan and Hindostan, which has generally intervened effectively to prevent the political subjection of the south to the north.

Of the rivers, it is to be noted that the Satlej has recently been found to be an effective boundary between the Panjab and the districts on its south and east: while the Nerbadda has been a nominal boundary between Hindostan and the Dekhan. The Warda, joining the Godaveri and flowing to the east coast, is a line of demarcation between a wild country of hills and jungles eastwards and the more cultivated and civilised portion of the Dekhan plateau westwards. Further south, the Tănghăbădra and the Krishna set the limits to the Northward movements of aggressors from Mysore. The richest land in India is the basin of the Ganges—Ganga, the holy stream.

Certain characteristics of the climate exercise an important influence on the sequence of events. Climate.

India is roughly speaking the size of Europe without Russia. Within that space there is room for considerable varieties of climate. In the north, the thermometer sometimes touches freezing point by night in the cold season: while on the plains in the hot weather the heat becomes extreme. In the Dekhan the temperature is more equable. But in the south there is less cold season, the hot weather setting in in March while in the Panjab it does not set in till May.

In the Panjab and to some degree on the upper Ganges, the mean level of the country is fairly high, and the heat is fierce but dry till the rains come; in Bengal, where the level is low, the air is moist and the heat more enervating. From the end of May till September south-westerly winds blow, called the monsoons, bringing with them the rains: rain in quantities entirely beyond European experience. Except for the modification introduced by artificial irrigation, the productiveness of the country depends entirely on the rains, and their failure means inevitable famine. In the North West, the monsoons coming less off the ocean, bring with them less water. In the Dekhan, caught by the Western Ghăts, much of the rainfall is exhausted before the eastern plains are reached: but over Hindostan it is distributed fairly evenly. The hot season interferes greatly with military operations, especially for European troops; when the rains set in, active operations are often rendered almost impossible.

In October, a sort of counter-monsoon begins blowing from the North East, giving the south-eastern coasts their rainfall, though not so lavishly as the south-western monsoons elsewhere. The whole stretch of the east coast below Bengal being very deficient in harbourage, naval operations are liable to be brought to a standstill while the counter monsoon is blowing from October to December.

Races and languages. From these geographical conditions certain results follow. Primitive populations tend to be forced back into the hilly regions by immigrant hordes of different race. The immigrants come always by the same route, through the Suleiman mountains, across the Panjab, and then spread themselves over all Hindostan. The primitive peoples are absorbed or enslaved, but make their stand at the passes into the Dekhan, where they hold their own very much as the Celtic populations maintained their resistance to the Teutonic invaders in Wales, and in the Highlands of Scotland. Hence the languages of the Dekhan—Tamil, Telugu, Canarese—are pre-Aryan tongues; although the later invaders who did succeed in making good their footing in these regions, introduced also the modified language, Urdu or Hindostani, the language of the camp, which is a sort of composite chiefly of Hindi (the purest offspring of Sanskrit) and Persian—the last having become the prevailing language of the eastern peoples for mutual intercourse very much as French achieved a like position though a less universal one in Europe.

Invaders. Many centuries before the Christian era, a branch of the great Aryan or Indo-European race descended upon Hindostan, subjugating or expelling the earlier inhabitants, and introducing the religion, the laws, and the language of the conquerors. The Hindu advance was checked by the mountains and jungles of the northern Dekhan, into which their supremacy never seems to have penetrated, though curiously enough their religion did. It is probable that there were subsequent Scythian incursions, but these invaders were absorbed, subjugated, or assimilated, by their Hindu predecessors. The descent of Alexander was a unique episode, introducing no permanent Occidentalism into the East, no continued intercourse of East and West. The actual records of Hindu history are about ninety-nine parts myth to one part fact, which affords a large field for hypothetical reconstruction; but after Mohammed arose, the warriors who carried the banner of Islam into the land of the Hindus were accompanied by chroniclers whose historical perceptions were doubtless defective, but who recognised a marked distinction between recording facts and inventing fables. These conquerors carried their arms from end to end of Hindostan, and established monarchies over great part of the Dekhan. The Moslem invasions culminated with the establishment of the Mogul or Mughal empire in the sixteenth century A.D.; the hordes of Nadir Shah and Ahmed Shah Durāni, a couple of hundred years afterwards, neglecting to secure any permanent foothold.

The Indian People. Now we can observe the elements of which is constructed the India known to the Western race which was destined in its turn to acquire a new supremacy over the peoples of the East. First, the great pre-Aryan population of various types, speaking varying tongues, worshipping ancestors, native gods, devils innumerable, with every variety of primitive rite. Then a conquering Aryan race, always probably a minority of the population, establishing itself as a ruling patrician class all over Hindostan, professing and enforcing a religion pantheistic in idea but suggestive of a refined nature-worship in fact, of which the influence extends over the unconquered portion of the peninsula. Then an admixture of warlike barbarian tribes who do not predominate but are absorbed. Hence throughout the fertile plains of Hindostan, the development of a civilisation very far from contemptible, accompanied by the gradual evolution of religion in two very different directions—one esoteric, mystical ascetic, reserved to the initiated, the other popular, gross idolatrous, deformed by pre-historic superstitions; not without its parallel in the absorption by primitive Christianity of pagan imaginings which it had failed to eradicate. And then, century by century, wave after wave of fanatical Mussulman conquerors, Arab and Persian, Pathān and Turki and Tartar, whose political ideal is conquest for its own sake, save when there arises now and again a Sher Shah or an Akbar with larger conceptions: Mussulmans and Hindus always remaining separate though not absolutely without admixture; while the former necessarily retain the character of a military caste, amongst a more or less subject population outnumbering them by four or five to one.

Hinduism: Caste.

The Hindu religion has changed very considerably, as we have noted, from the form in which it is presented in the early sacred books known as the Vedas. The institution which has always appeared to be most essentially characteristic of it is *Caste*. This may be described as the permanent division of the whole Hindu society into hereditary classes, whose intercourse with each other is restricted under a religious sanction: demanding the strictest fulfilment of all manner of rites and observances on pain of losing caste, and deriving its tremendous influence from the conviction that caste extends to the life beyond the grave, controlling the transmigration and re-incarnations of the soul. Primarily, all Hindus fall into two categories—the "Twice-born" and the rest; which the learned seem on the whole to agree in regarding as a race-distinction between the Aryan and his predecessor. The Twice-born, again, are in three divisions: the Brahmin or priestly caste, the Kshātrўas (otherwise Rajputs) or military, and the Vaisyas or industrial. The rest are Sūdras, not precisely slaves but altogether inferior. These may be called the four original Castes. The basis of division is the hereditary distinction of function, maintained by the impassable character of the barrier between one caste and another. There is a time during which the Kshatryas challenge the supremacy of the Brahmins, but the attempt fails. It is a curious point that the law against intermarriage is not absolute. A man may take a wife from a lower caste—not indeed without penalty, but without complete degradation; but a woman must marry in her own caste or above it.

Caste in modern times.

Naturally, the Brahmins to whom the caste-distinction was of the greatest consequence maintained their purity of caste with greater accuracy and remain at least almost pure-blooded * to this day. With the others extreme strictness appears to have been periodically relaxed, and the Brahmins are apt to deny that any of the rest have remained pure, though Rajputs declare themselves to be pure Kshatryas. Throughout Hindostan there are now races or castes, such

* There is some doubt whether the Brahmins of the Dekhan are pure Brahmins, or descended from progenitors who were allowed to amalgamate with the unconquered non-Aryan Dekhanis without losing caste.

as the Jhats, who account themselves very little lower than Rajputs. The Marathas on the other hand, are said to be almost entirely low-caste, though some claim a Rajput descent, and Brahmins have held a large share in their government. But the practical result is, that whereas of the four original castes the Brahmins remain, the Rajputs or Kshatryas have been little modified, while the rest have become indistinguishable; yet among all, distinction of hereditary function and also of locality have been carried to such a pitch that there are now some hundreds of castes for which intermarriage, eating together, and other details of social intercourse, are forbidden under various pains and penalties; while to all the out-caste or non-Hindu is unclean, and to all the person of a Brahmin is sacred.

Other religions. Buddhism, a variant which sprung out of Brahminism in India, and spread over the East, becoming the recognised religion of Chinese, Tibetans, and Burmese, was also for a time dominant in India itself, but finally gave place again to the religion which it had attempted to supplant; so that apart from Christianity practically all natives of India are either professing Hindus or professing Mohammedans. One Hindu sect, that of the Sikhs, who reject the religious validity of caste altogether, has played an important part in history, more particularly during the last century and a half; but their unorthodoxy has not separated them from the Hindu body. To the Mussulmans, all alike are idolaters; while to all Hindus the Mussulman is out-caste and unclean equally with the Christian.

Indian Nationality. From these considerations we can derive a comparatively definite idea of what may be meant by Indian Nationality. A territory as large as Europe without Russia: in which the population is everywhere practically divided between two religions extremely hostile to each other in character: with races and languages as divergent as those of the Celt, the Teuton, the Roman, and the Slav: which at no period known to history has been organized as one State;—this is not a nation at all in the sense in which we distinguish the nations of Europe. In the eyes of an Oriental, it would be much easier to distinguish and class at sight a Bengali

Brahmin, a Sikh, a Ghurka, and a Marātha, than a Frenchman, an Englishman, a Spaniard, and an Austrian. The religious antagonism between the Calvinist and the Romanist is nothing compared with that between the devout followers of Vishnu or Khali and the followers of the Arab prophet.

But the distinction between East and West is more than between nation and nation, or between creed and creed. Peoples who have no sense of unity will become united to resist a more intensely alien force. The Maratha is more akin to the Pathan than to the Englishman; as the Englishman is more akin to the Frenchman than to the Maratha. There are Indian habits of mind as there are European habits of mind. We cannot quite formulate the distinction as one between Orientalism and Occidentalism, for the Chinaman is an Oriental who is hardly if at all more akin to the Indian than is the European. If we had a term to distinguish the Brown from the Yellow Oriental, generalisation would be easier to express and less liable to misapprehension when formulated. The East has its two great divisions, which are little better adapted for amalgamation than the Indian and the European. The primary facts to be grasped however are two: the Indo-orientals, Pathans, Rajputs, Bengalis, or Marathas, may be opposed to each other as Frenchmen and Germans or English may be; but the opposition is insignificant in comparison to that subsisting between all of them and the European; just as the type-distinctions of European nations become insignificant in comparison to that between all of them and the Indo-oriental. Europe might, imaginably, be formed into a Commonwealth—one federation of autonomous states: India actually is a Dominion, an Empire, where one supreme government controls subordinate States: but it needs a powerful and untrammelled imagination to conceive of either India or Europe as a State, single, centralised and homogeneous.

The British Conquest.

Similarly it is a mere parody of history, as we shall see, to talk of the British, led by Clive, having overthrown a mighty Empire; unless the Nawab of Bengal is to be called an Emperor.

Before Clive's time, the Mogul Empire had already ceased to subsist except as a legal fiction: as a legal fiction, it continued to subsist for nearly half a century after the conquest of Bengal.

One after another, in the course of a hundred years, the kingdoms and confederacies of India fell under British dominion. But a clear century passed between the time when the game of king-making was begun by Dupleix in the Carnatic, and that when British dominion was extended to Peshawar; though each step forward might be called a stride, the process was one of gradual advance; of the successive overthrow of Powers which had flung down the gage of battle. When the contest began, the Mogul empire—the only one which ever had any pretension to extend its sway over the whole peninsula, and which might fairly be said only to have clutched at Universal dominion without grasping it—was a mere congeries of practically independent principalities. And when the great upheaval came in 1857, one at least of the most potent causes which held back the native princes from joining it was the revelation of the intention of a section of its most active promoters to use it for a Mogul restoration. India did not take up arms against the British for a national idea; the peoples of India had never possessed a common national idea. So far as there was a common motive force, it was entirely negative and destructive. Had the mutiny been successful, it would not have established a new Empire in India, but a collection of warring races and factions. Great Britain has never pursued the policy of the phrase "*Divide et impera.*" The tendency of her rule is in fact to reduce the impossibility of union for a single political end by a gradual elimination of discordant factors: a course which will supply the political philosopher of a hundred years hence with very interesting material. The British Rāj in India is the most gigantic political experiment that the world has known: its outcome still lies upon the knees of the gods.

CHAPTER II

MOHAMMEDAN DOMINION

(*Maps I. and II.*)

India before Mohammed. WHEN the prophet of Arabia arose and kindled the torch of Islam, India was a congeries of Hindu kingdoms. Throughout Hindostan, the military and quasi-military functions, including those of royalty, were roughly all in the hands of Rajputs and the administrative in those of Brahmins, while in the Dekhan these two superior castes were comparatively little represented, though held in due respect. The Rajputs were not, and are not now confined to Rajputana; which is the name given to the great district in the West, which remained under Rajput dominion, and was never brought into complete subjection by Mohammedan conquerors. The rise of Mohammedanism in western and central Asia led to the series of Moslem conquests culminating early in the sixteenth century with that of Bāber, the founder of the so-called Mogul dynasty.

Mohammed launched the Arabs on a career of conquest which extended their Empire to Spain on the West, and over Persia on the East; and spread their religion till it was embraced by the Afghans and Bilūchis lying between Persia and India, and by two of the three great divisions of the Tartar race occupying central India. With the third of these, the Manchus, who made themselves masters of China, Indian history has no concern; the other two, the Turks and the Mughāls play an important part in Indian affairs.

The first year of the Mohammedan era, commonly called the Hegira, is the year 622 A.D. Within a century, the Arabs had themselves crossed the Indus; but they obtained no foothold. Islam had been enthusiastically adopted by races whose religion was effete, but it did not offer the same attractions to peoples whose own faith was a lively reality. The natives of India never accepted it save at the point of the sword; and a stronger impulse to conquest than that which inspired the Arabs was required to subdue Hindostan by force of arms.

Mahmud of Ghazni.

From time immemorial, it has been a recognised custom in the east for monarchs to elevate capable slaves into provincial governors. It has also been the custom for them to depend largely on slave or mercenary troops drawn from fighting tribes beyond their own actual dominions. Towards the close of the tenth century, a Turk slave named Alptegin, made governor of Afghanistan, established himself as an independent sovereign, with an army composed partly of Turks and partly of Afghans. His successor was another Turk slave to whom he gave his daughter in marriage; and their son was the famous Mahmud of Ghazni.

Between the years 1000 and 1030 Mahmud made twelve expeditions into India, carrying his arms to Somnāth in Gujerat (whence he took away the sandal-wood gates of a great Hindu shrine, whereof more was heard in 1842), and to Kanauj half-way between Lucknow and Agra. He came, however, not to stay but to collect treasure and to spread the Mohammedan faith. It was not till the last quarter of the following century that the Ghōri dynasty—probably Afghan—founded a Mohammedan dominion in India.

Successive Mussulman dynasties.

Between 1176 and 1206, Mohammed Ghori, otherwise called Shahāb-ud-din, conquered all the countries of the Ganges basin, with much of Rajputana. An entire Rajput clan migrated bodily in consequence from Kanauj to Jōdpūr. The Ghori dominion broke up into separate kingdoms almost immediately. Another dynasty, taking its rise from a Turk slave of Shahab-ud-din, took up the reins of empire at Delhi. These "slave" emperors practically end with the energetic, but unattractive Balban; whose successor made way in 1288 for a fresh dynasty, the Khilji, of Afghan stock. During the next five and twenty years, the Delhi empire which already included the whole of Hindostan with varying degrees of effectiveness was extended by Ala-ud-dīn over most of the Dekhan. His successor was dethroned in a revolt which again raised a Turk family to the highest place. This, the Tughlak dynasty, brought a larger share of the whole peninsula under Mohammedan dominion than could be claimed even for Aurangzīb; but the success was short-lived. Before 1350, a part of the Dekhan had reverted to its Hindu princes, and the whole of it as well as Bengal, was in revolt against the Delhi monarchy. The collapse of the Empire was completed by the devastating invasion of Timur or Tamerlane in 1398. For a century and a quarter thereafter there was no really dominant power in India. In Hindostan some Rajput princes recovered complete independence; the Delhi government fell into the hands of a Seiad dynasty (*i.e.* a family claiming descent from the Prophet) for fifty years, and then into those of the Lōdi (Afghan) dynasty, who once more added the Panjab and Sirhind to the surviving fraction of the old empire. Elsewhere, in Gujerat, in Malwa, in Bengal, Mohammedans retained the supremacy, but in separate monarchies. In the Dekhan for some time after the revolt from the Tughlaks the Mohammedan "Bhāmăni" dynasty was the chief power, with the Hindu kingdom of Bijanagar (Beejanugger) or Vizayanagar on the west holding second place. During the fifteenth century, the Bhamanis extended their dominion over the Hindus; but early in the next century the kingdom broke up into the three main Mohammedan States of Bijapur, Ahmednagar (Ahmednugger) and Golconda, and two minor ones.

Mohammedans before Baber. With the coming of Baber in 1524 a new era may be said to commence. From the first successes of Shahab-ud-din (Mohammed Ghori) in 1193 to Baber's invasion, no fresh conqueror had led victorious armies into Hindostan save Tamerlane; who had appeared and disappeared merely, like a devastating pestilence. A Mohammedan empire had been established. Its successive dynasties, Afghan or Turk, had wrested the government from each other, but each had arisen within the empire. Their dominion, extending at an early stage over most of Hindostan, was carried into the

Dekhan; and then Mussulman generals and governors set themselves up as independent potentates, resting their power mainly on armies composed of Turks, Mughals, and Afghans, exacting revenues from their Hindu subjects. The process of Moslem conquest was simple. Professedly its primary intent was the spread of Islam. It offered to the infidel the three alternatives—conversion, tribute, or death. When it was resisted, victory was followed by the slaughter of the fighting men, and sweeping measures of enslavement for their women and children. Those who yielded timely submission, were treated as subjects, not on an equality with the conquerors; still they were spared the merciless treatment meted out to those who resisted. But everywhere, to the Hindus, the Turks or Mughals or Afghans alike were foreign conquerors of an alien and detested religion.

Thus when Baber came, he was not a Moslem smiting or subduing the infidel, but a Moslem overthrowing Moslem Powers. The amalgamation of the invaders and the invaded—of the new and the old Mohammedan ruling classes—was an easy matter. Mohammedan dominion was again organised; but again its extension beyond Hindostan was soon followed by disruption, and the Mogul Empire would have given place, in all probability, to a recovered Hindu ascendancy, but for the introduction into India of the new European factor.

Ever since the establishment of the Arab Empire, the Turk and Mughal divisions of the Tartar race had supplied dynasties and mercenary troops for the various kingdoms which rose and fell in Western and Central Asia. Early in the thirteenth century, about the time when in England the barons were extorting the Great Charter from John, the Mughals under Chenghis, Jenghis, or Zenghis Khan, swept over half the Eastern world slaughtering and burning; happily for India, they left it practically alone. Less than two centuries later, Tamerlane the Turk, with hordes of Turks and Mughals, emulated the deeds of Jenghis Khan, incidentally falling upon Hindostan. Tamerlane's descendants held among them vast territories in central Asia; of whom one was Baber, born of a Mughal mother in 1482. His figure stands out in the page of history, picturesque,

The Tartars.

Baber.

romantic, fascinating; a soldier and a poet, revelling in adventure, buoyant of spirit in adversity, generous in prosperity, rejoicing in deeds of prowess and at the same time enjoying the society of men of wit and wisdom. His large humanity did not indeed lift him entirely clear of the inhumanities which were to be taken for granted in every Asiatic conqueror, and more particularly in any Tartar; his attitude on such points as the slaughter of stubborn opponents must be compared not with contemporary European standards but with those of the days of Charlemagne. He did not organise the empire he won; but the winning of it was a brilliant achievement the work of a born leader and a singularly attractive personality.

The Lodi Kings of Delhi had extended their sway over the Panjab to the North West and Behar on the East: but Oudh, Behar and the Panjab all revolted. Baber, after adventures enough, between the ages of twelve and twenty-four, to satisfy for life half a dozen potentates of mature age, had found himself king of Kābŭl in 1506: after a variety of further vicissitudes he was still king of Kabul when in 1524 the revolting governor of the Panjab invited his assistance. Baber promptly responded to the invitation, invading and taking possession of the Panjab; but he found it necessary to return to Kabul, leaving a lieutenant who advanced against Delhi, but was severely defeated. In December, Baber returned with an army of only 12,000 men; shattered at Pānipat the Delhi monarch's troops, which outnumbered his own by something like ten to one; and in May 1525 was master of Delhi and Agra. Those chief, however, who had already been more or less in revolt against the Lodi King were in no hurry to acquiesce in the domination of Baber and the small army, very unlike the vast hordes of Tamerlane, which he had brought with him. But Baber's troops, encouraged by a tone and spirit on the part of their commander which find an apt parallel in those of Edward III. at Crecy, and of Henry V. at Agincourt, stood by him loyally; successes brought submission and fresh adherents; and before the end of the following year, all the Mussulman territories that had owned submission to the

Baber invades India.

Delhi kings accepted the rule of the Turk, misnamed Mughal, who founded the dynasty known to the English as that of the Moguls.

Now however the independent Rajput princes of Rajputana and Malwa continued to do battle with the new monarchy. The armies met and lay facing each other at Sikri, some twenty miles from Agra; a panic was all but created among the Tartar forces by an astrologer who proclaimed that the planets foretold their certain destruction, but again Baber appealed to their chivalry with success; every man swore to conquer or to die; and they conquered. The rest of that year and of the year following were occupied in establishing the Mogul government on the borders and in Oudh and Behar. In 1529, Bengal also was added to Baber's dominions, and in 1530 he died, being succeeded by his son Humayūn.

In six years Baber, had made himself lord of nearly all of Hindostan; but the achievement was mainly due to his own unique personality; elements of stability were conspicuously wanting in the empire which his son inherited. Humayun Humayūn. had brothers who also according to Oriental custom, disputed the succession and succeeded in appropriating Kabul. He then became engaged in a war with Gujerāt; and in the meantime a noble of the Afghan stock, Shēr Khān (soon to become Sher Shah) got possession of Behar and Bengal. When Humayun was free from the Gujerat complication, he marched against Sher Shah; but the latter avoided facing his full strength in the field until the Mogul army began to grow demoralised; and then by unusually skilful strategical and tactical moves succeeded in surprising him and scattering his army. Later on Sher Shah again inflicted on him so serious a defeat that he had to make his way to Kabul as a fugitive (1540).

For the next five years, Sher Shah reigned and reigned well in Hindostan, anticipating Akbar's methods; for ten more his successors reigned ill. The provinces revolted; Humayun after fifteen years of exile, made his way back to India and recovered Delhi and Agra. But he had hardly returned when he met with a fatal accident; and Akbar, the greatest of the Moguls ascended the throne, being thirteen years of age (1556).

The affairs of the rival monarchy were curiously enough in the hands of a Hindu minister of low caste, who showed conspicuous ability and valour. But Bairam, the young Akbar's guardian, was a Turkman of tried capacity; the army of the Afghan dynasty with its Hindu leader was met and vanquished at Panipat, a very favourite battlefield: the Panjab had already been subdued; and the house of Timur (Tamerlane) was once more dominant by force of arms in Hindostan.

Akbar. Akbar came to the throne two years before the accession of Elizabeth in England; he died two years after her. The reigns of his son and grandson covered another half century; that of Aurangzib fifty years more, a quite extraordinary period for four generations of rulers, though just exceeded by Henry III. of England and his three successors. It was the glory of Akbar that he was no mere conqueror, but the real creator of a true and majestic empire such as India had never known; not the mere military despotism of a conquering race, but a rule under which the Hindu and the Mussulman found approximately equal scope. It was reserved for Aurangzib to desert his great ancestor's policy and, by reverting to a militant Mohammedanism, to destroy the scheme of unity which it was Akbar's chief aim to foster.

During the first years of Akbar's reign, until he reached the age of eighteen, the government was ably but arrogantly administered by Bairam, who recovered the Imperial territory as far east as Behār, as well as the districts of Malwa bordering on the Jamna provinces. At the age of eighteen, Akbar suddenly asserted himself, and terminated the period of his tutelage, showing much magnanimity towards the fallen minister; who however was shortly afterwards assassinated by a private enemy.

In the circumstances in which the young monarch found himself, the mere maintenance of a military despotism would have been a task demanding unusual ability. Of the Mussulmans in his dominions, a great proportion were Afghans, favouring an Afghan dynasty in preference to the

Moguls. The Hindus regarded Moguls and Afghans impartially as foreign conquerors. Akbar's own dynasty had begun with Baber, who had himself only entered India some five and thirty years before; while Humayun had passed fifteen of the intervening years in exile. His grandfather's military exploits were an inadequate basis for Akbar's empire over Hindostan to rest upon. Carried on according to the old lines, the reign would have resolved itself into an endless series of revolts, probably ending with a struggle for the succession between the sons of the monarch, and a subversion of the dynasty at an early date.

Akbar's policy.

Akbar however, invented a policy, foreshadowed by Sher Shah, but otherwise unprecedented in Hindostan: a policy not so much of dominion as of union. It was his normal practice, when Afghans or Rajputs set him at defiance, first to crush their resistance and then to give their chiefs high rank in the empire. Sometimes, a chief would take advantage of this magnanimity to plot further revolts: but in general the effect was to convert enemies into loyal supporters. In particular, the Rajput princes with the exception of the irreconcilable Rāna of Udaipur (Oodeypore) found themselves adopting an entirely new attitude. Instead of being under the dominion of Afghan and Turk governors and armies, they became themselves princes of the Empire. Their daughters were numbered among the wives of the Imperial family; they themselves commanded the imperial armies and administered the imperial provinces. The Hindu ceased to be taxed for not being a Mussulman. The intolerance of Islam, officially mitigated by a monarch who was ready to listen to and argue with Brahmin *pandits* and Jesuit missionaries, became unofficially also greatly relaxed. Akbar chose his servants with immense skill, and the revenue arrangements made by Tōdar Mal—himself a Hindu—diminished the burden of taxation while greatly increasing the Imperial receipts.

Given oriental conditions to work in, Akbar appears to have more nearly realised the Platonic conception of the philosopher-king than any monarch of history, except Marcus Aurelius. Baber had been almost an ideal mediæval knight.

Akbar was a modern in mediæval surroundings; great as a soldier, great as a statesman, a thinker of no mean order; personally brave with the most daring, generous and humane beyond the highest standards of his day. By the time that he was fifty years old, all Hindostan with Kabul beyond the mountains formed one vast organised dominion, throughout which something very like equal government and equal rights prevailed for Hindus and Mussulmans.

Results of his rule. Akbar failed in a long effort to bring under his rule the mountain tribes of that northern frontier, which at this day is hardly under the control of the British government. On the other hand, he became during the last twelve years of his life engaged in wars in the Dekhan, which resulted in the annexation of Khandēsh and part of Berār; but the three great Mohammedan kingdoms of Ahmednagar, Bijapur, and Golconda remained independent, to be only by degrees overthrown during the next hundred years.

The empire which passed to the successor of Akbar on the great king's death in 1605 was a mighty heritage, embracing more than half India. The vast territory was divided into governorships, none of them large enough to offer inducements for attempts at independence. The enlightenment of the monarch had placed a check on extravagantly inhuman practices, such as the compulsory self-immolation of widows among the Hindus, while it had protected them from interference with their less objectionable observances, and had raised their status in relation to the dominant Mohammedan races. Taxation had been reduced, and the tyranny of local or provincial magnates brought under restraint.

Jehangir. The accession of the king's son, Selim, now known as Jehāngir, hardly gave promise of a continuation of such beneficent government; for the new ruler had shown unmistakable signs of a cruel disposition, and a taste for debauchery. Happily however, he had not been long on the throne, when he married the celebrated Nūr Jehān, who exercised over him a supreme, and usually most salutary influence.

In fact the reign of Jehangir was not conspicuous either for increase of territory or development of organisation.

In Hindostan, Akbar's principles of administration were maintained, though probably the whole moral atmosphere and the ethical standards of governors and officers were lowered. The Imperial pomp and magnificence gave the tone to the nobility, and European travellers found not a little to admire, while they were struck by the venality of officials. In the Dekhan, throughout the reign, Ahmednagar under the government of an Abyssinian minister named Malik Amber maintained its position successfully, its ruler proving in the game of war, a match for the Mogul commanders, except Prince Khărram, later known as Shah Jehan. Before he was five and twenty, this prince showed extraordinary abilities both political and military. But the inherent weakness of all oriental monarchies became apparent when the queen Nur Jehan began to intrigue against his succession. From 1620 Shah Jehan (who had already been granted the royal title) was in perpetual revolt, or on the verge of it, not with the design of displacing his father, but in self-defence; and although on the Emperor's death, in 1627, he established himself on the throne with little difficulty, he in his turn, found thirty years later that the precedent of filial disobedience is one which the next generation is particularly ready to copy.

Shah Jehan.

The death of Malik Amber shortly before that of Jehangir altered the relations between the Dekhan and the empire of Hindostan. The kingdom of Ahmednagar under a less capable ruler than the Abyssinian, could neither avoid collision with the Mogul, nor resist his armies; and the reign of Shah Jehan saw the ruin of that kingdom and the partition of its territory between the Empire and the astute prince of Bijapur; who turned the contest to his own advantage, while the less skilful monarch of Golconda found himself compelled to pay a heavy tribute to the Mogul. During the war with Ahmednagar, the name of a Maratha chief for the first time appears prominently. This was Shahji Bhonsla, whose son Sīvaji was the founder of Maratha greatness. Shahji supported the dynasty of Ahmednagar till the cause had become entirely hopeless; after which he became attached to Bijapur.

This war was finished before Shah Jehan had been reigning ten years, and for a considerable time thereafter the only serious military operations were carried on beyond the Afghan frontier of India, where the future monarch Aurangzib learned some of the unpleasant lessons of failure. Transferred to the Dekhan, his armies met with more success, and the crooked methods of his policy found scope. In 1657, Shah Jehan fell ill; the usual antagonism among the sons who were each of them prepared to bid for the succession arose: and Aurangzib made up his own mind that the question would be best settled by his own occupation of the throne, and the deposition of his father. This plan he carried out in the course of 1658 from which date his reign begins. Shah Jehan was simply deprived of power, but otherwise was treated with respect and honour for the remaining years of his life.

The Mogul zenith. When the deposed Shah Jehan had succeeded his father at the age of thirty-seven, he had already for fifteen years been constantly and honourably engaged in war, in administration, and in diplomacy: and latterly he had been ill-rewarded. When the sceptre of the Moguls fell definitely into his hands, he proved a less strenuous ruler than might have been expected from his earlier record; perhaps because he now had the opportunity for gratifying other tastes. He had no craving for conquest; nor did he change the methods of administration. Nevertheless, he was by no means unworthy to be the grandson of Akbar. Until the latter days when his sons began to dispute about the succession, peace reigned within the wide borders of Hindostan itself. He did not fully maintain the policy of equality for Hindus and Mussulmans; but his departure from it was not very grave: under him, Hindostan obtained a high pitch of prosperity, the highest it had known. Hence, although no additional burdens were laid upon his subjects, the imperial revenues were greatly enhanced; and while there was no curtailment of the expenditure on public works of utility, an immense outlay on mere magnificence was rendered possible without diminishing the balance in the imperial treasury. The cities of Hindostan obtained an unprecedented splendour; it was the wealth of Shah Jehan that constructed the famous Peacock Throne; to him India owes many of the wonderful buildings which have excited the astonished admiration of so many travellers, and most of all the incomparable Moti Masjid or Pearl Mosque, and the Taj Mahal, the mausoleum of his favourite wife, at Agra. The highest panegyrics of the Mohammedan historians are reserved for the Mohammedan zealot Aurangzib; Akbar the liberal and unorthodox creator of the Empire demands universal admiration however grudging; but the golden age of the Mogul dominion is the reign of Shah Jehan.

Aurangzib.

But in the East, though a great man build up a noble empire, and his son and his son's son maintain it, so soon as the sceptre falls into incapable hands, dynasty and empire crumble together. Shah Jehan's successor maintained the empire and enlarged its borders—but in so doing he prepared the way to make its collapse the more complete and irretrievable.

CHAPTER III

THE MOGUL DISRUPTION AND THE MARATHAS

(*Maps I. and II.*)

The great Moguls. THROUGHOUT the three great reigns last chronicled, the effective extent of the Mogul dominion in India corresponds practically with what we have called Greater Hindostan; Mohammedan dynasties at Ahmednagar, Bijapur, and Golconda dominating the Dekhan. Both in Hindostan and the Dekhan the tendency to religious toleration had been fairly maintained; and though *ceteris paribus* the Mussulman was preferred to the Hindu by the ruling powers, the latter was by no means excluded from offices of honour, responsibility and emolument, nor could it fairly be said that the Hindu religion suffered definite persecution.

Elements of disintegration. In the eyes of faithful Mohammedans Aurangzib is the greatest of his line. Others find that both the ends which he set before himself and the methods by which he pursued them led directly to that collapse of the Mogul Power which followed immediately on his death; and that the revival of militant Hinduism, which had almost disappeared for a century, made use of and was fostered by the emperor's intolerant Mohammedanism, associated with his aggressively destructive policy towards the Mohammedan kingdoms of the south. In grasping at the Dekhan, he extended the bounds of the Empire too far for efficient control by the central power, while the Hindu Marathas utilised the strife of their nominal over-lords to develop a power which before the middle of the eighteenth century had become at least as formidable as any existing Moslem State. To the same period, and largely to the same intolerant attitude on the part of the Emperor, must be ascribed the formation of the disciples of the Hindu reformer Nanuk, in the North West into a fighting sect under the Guru Govind Singh; whereof later on came important developments; the Sikhs of the Panjab becoming a barrier against Afghan incursions, and then an organised State which in its turn challenged the British dominion, and has subsequently after annexation supplied our armies with many of their most trusty troops. Unlike the Marathas, however, the Sikhs do not become a recognised factor in the situation till the close of the eighteenth century. Their growth will form the subject of a later chapter: we have here to follow the aggressive and disintegrating policy of Aurangzib, the growth of the Marathas, and the breaking up of the unwieldy Empire into great provinces, nominally subject to the Mogul or Padishah at Delhi, really independent sovereign States; with whom we were to fight or over whom we were to extend our protection, until according to circumstances, they were ultimately absorbed into the Protectorate or the Dominion of Great Britain.

Aurangzib's first years.

The accession of Aurangzib (1658) and the deposition of Shah Jehan were followed according to Oriental custom by a period of contested successions. Three brothers, their sons, a son of his own, and the Rajput chiefs of Jeipur and Jodpur, with their varying combinations, kept Aurangzib (otherwise known as Alam Gir) fully occupied for some four years before his position was definitely secured; and possibly the remarkable courage, self-possession and resource which he displayed when suffering from a severe illness, went far in deciding waverers to support his cause. It was not, however, till he had been on the throne for more than twenty years that he began that series of campaigns in the Dekhan which, while adding greatly to the extent of his empire, made it practically impossible to preserve its integrity. But in the interval the lust of conquest made him pursue through his viceroys a policy in the Dekhan which weakened the Mohammedan states of Bijapur and Golconda, and thereby enabled the Maratha Sivaji to lay the foundations of a far more formidable Power; one, moreover, which being Hindu with Hindu sympathies, was infinitely more destructive of the Mogul supremacy throughout Hindostan itself. It is probable, however, that Aurangzib would have thrown his full energies into the suppression of Sivaji at an earlier date, but for the troublesome necessities of campaigns on the Afghan frontier where the methods and manners of the tribesmen were very much what they are to-day.

Aurangzib's Mohammedan fanaticism.

When this contest in the North was brought to an end, Aurangzib found himself involved, by the intolerant bigotry of his Mohammedan predilections, in a prolonged struggle with the Hindu Rajputs. In part the character of his innovations on the tolerant practice of his predecessors was something of the same kind as might have been found in the rule of an austere Puritan, set down to govern autocratically a population consisting mainly of Roman Catholics whose religious observances he regarded as idolatrous, and whose amusements he accounted as inventions of the Arch Enemy. But besides the decrees which were felt as insulting to the Hindu religion, he altered the incidence of taxation in accordance with the dictates of Mohammedan law; whereby relief was nominally given to large traders, though practically the revenue officers merely continued to enforce the charges while rendering no account of them; the taxes from which the commonalty suffered were left untouched: and presently he directly differentiated between Hindus and Mohammedans, by reducing the customs claims against the latter by one-half.

Then he went further, issuing to all his principal officers orders for the general exclusion of Hindus from appointments; and re-instituted the poll-tax on "infidels" which had originally been imposed as a kind of commutation of the alternative of death or conversion, but had been abolished at the beginning of Akbar's reign. These measures had the effect of creating general disaffection among the Hindus, and of strengthening their sympathy with the Marathas throughout the Dekhan; moreover in conjunction with another act of Aurangzib, they had the effect of permanently alienating practically all Rajputana, and turning the hitherto constant and loyal support of its chiefs into a hostility to the Moguls either latent or active. This act was the emperor's attempt to get into his own hands the widow and children of

Hindu antagonism.

Jeswănt Singh of Jodpur (who died at Kabul during the settlement of the Afghan troubles) on their way back through the Panjab. The Rajputs smuggled the Rani and the princes out of camp, and then fought stubbornly in professed defence of substitutes left behind in their place—whom Aurangzib afterwards made a point of treating as the genuine family of Jeswant Singh. Raj Singh of Udaipur threw in his lot with the Jodpur people; the Mogul marched armies against them with orders to burn and destroy, and to carry off women and children. The Rajputs retaliated by intriguing with his sons, and persuading one of them, Akbar, to revolt and join them. Akbar's army however was persuaded to return to its allegiance, and the prince made his way to the Maratha country as promising a more favourable field of operations; this being about the time of Sivaji's death (1680). The necessity of reducing the Dekhan had now become so important that Aurangzib patched up a peace with the Rajputs on terms which saved his credit, but nothing more; while their loyalty of a century had been finally and fatally destroyed.

The Maratha race.

Five and twenty years before, the Marathas had not begun to exist as a Power. The home of that race lies roughly within a mountainous triangle, having the West coast from Goa northwards to Kandesh as its base, and its apex near Nagpur; for the most part within the domains of Ahmednagar and Bijapur while those two monarchies were flourishing. The race, including its chiefs is of low caste, though here and there a claim with possible justification is put forward to an infusion of Rajput blood. The numerous Brahmins politically associated with them, are presumably of different race, duly and religiously honoured as Brahmins; having in one case of primary importance acquired political leadership, but being more often found in the character of ministers or diplomatists than in that of military chiefs.

Shahji Bhonsla.

The Marathas are little mentioned until the beginning of the seventeenth century, when they were beginning to acquire a high fighting reputation especially as light horse. At that time two of them, Jādū Rao and Mālōji Bhonsla were prominent soldiers in the service of Ahmednagar. Shahji

Bhonsla, son of the latter, was married to Jadu's daughter, the fruit of the union being Sivaji the founder of the Maratha power.

Shahji played an effective part and acquired large possessions, in the struggle of Ahmednagar against Shah Jehan. When the kingdom fell, the lands of Shahji and his services went to the kingdom of Bijapur, Shahji himself going to the *jaghīr* * granted to him at its southern extremity in Mysore, and leaving the young Sivaji to be educated on

Rise of Sivaji.

his northern jaghir at Puna. Here at a very early age the youth appears to have conceived the idea of gradually resuscitating a Hindu power, by the ostensible process of merely securing a strong strategical position for himself among the hills, without any actual appearance of treasonous designs against the Bijapur sovereignty. His methods, however, carried him a good deal further than seemed compatible with loyalty; his father remonstrated in vain, and was punished for his failure by suspicion and imprisonment. Sivaji thereupon sought protection for himself and intervention on behalf of his father from Shah Jehan, and obtained it. Shahji was formally released to attend to affairs in Mysore, and Sivaji promptly renewed his aggressive action in the North; maintaining, in spite of a premature incursion into Mogul territories, the fiction of loyalty to the Empire.

Just about the time when Aurangzib was occupied in dethroning Shah Jehan, Sivaji dealt a tremendous blow to Bijapur by decoying an army which the monarch had sent against him into the mountain defiles, on pretext of submission, and there falling on and slaughtering them after treacherously assassinating their commander with his own hand. The instrument with which the deed was done is known as the "tiger's claw"—a sharp steel claw concealed in the assassin's hand, and thrust into the victim in the act of embracing. Overwhelming forces were sent to punish him, but he evaded capture; revolts in other parts of the kingdom drew the royal army off; and in 1662 his father Shahji succeeded in negotiating terms which left him master of a territory about half the size of Great Britain, with a

* *Jaghir*: an estate held on condition of military service.

population eminently fitted to provide an army of the most serviceable type, and numbering more than fifty thousand fighting men—the nucleus of the great Maratha dominion.

Sivaji's exploits.

Sivaji had hardly made his peace with Bijapur when he was again moved to turn his arms against the Mogul territories. The imperial commander, Shaista Khan, marched from Aurangabad to chastise his insolence, and took possession of Puna (Poonah). The Maratha however with a small escort contrived to enter the town along with a marriage procession, made for the house where the general was to be found, surprised it, and all but captured Shaista Khan himself, besides slaying his son and most of his attendants. Having accomplished this feat, he successfully effected his retirement; winning by the performance much popularity and applause, and also causing a serious quarrel between the Khan and Jeswant Singh of Jodpur who had reinforced him. Sivaji followed up his success by a raid to the north-west and the looting of Surat; though his attack on the European factories there was repelled. Moreover, he employed himself in fitting out a fleet with which he raided the southern ports of Bijapur; and set himself up as an independent sovereign, with Raighar, near Puna, as his capital, coining money and assuming the title of Raja. Jey Singh another of the Rajputana princes was now sent by Aurangzib to suppress Sivaji and go on to attack Bijapur; and the Maratha, thinking the enemy too strong, at once set about making terms. The results were exceedingly favourable; for while he was obliged to surrender more than half his forts with the territories attached, and to hold the remainder not as an independent kingdom, but as a jaghir from the Mogul, he was compensated by a somewhat indefinite grant of claims on the revenues of Bijapur districts, which were subsequently found to be most conveniently elastic.

Sivaji negotiates.

Sivaji and Aurangzib.

The services which he rendered in the following Bijapur campaign were succeeded by a highly characteristic episode. Aurangzib invited him to Delhi, and he went, probably feeling very well pleased with himself. The invitation, however, expressed the limit of the emperor's condescension;

and his reception was not only cold but contemptuous. His protests were not taken in good part, and he soon found himself practically a prisoner. Feeling the risks of the situation, he succeeded in getting himself carried through the lines of sentinels concealed in a basket, took horse, and then travelling in various disguises succeeded in reaching his own country nine months after his escape from Delhi. Jey Singh's operations in Bijapur miscarried, and the Raja himself died; being replaced by a prince of the blood, associated with Jeswant Singh. The Jodpur Raja being always particularly well disposed towards Hindus, used his influence to obtain fresh terms for Sivaji, of a still more favourable character than before; including the restoration of a part of the confiscated territory, the grant of a new jaghir in Berar, and the recognition of his title as Raja.

Reconciliation.

Sivaji used this period of professed reconciliation with the emperor, first to threaten the kingdoms of Bijapur and Golconda, which preferred paying a tribute to fighting; and secondly to organise his own government which was highly systematised; all the principal civil and several of the military posts being in the hands of Brahmins.

Aurangzib's friendliness was however of a deceptive character, his real object being to draw Sivaji into his power again without actual war. But Jeswant Singh and the prince Moazzim, were quite capable of playing a double game, and it was not long before both sides were aware that duplicity was at work. Consequently Aurangzib at last decided on open war as the better course.

Successful defiance.

The results were decidedly favourable to Sivaji; who captured a number of forts, notably the apparently inaccessible one of Singhar, near Puna, and again ravaged Mogul territory as far north as Surat which he plundered for the second time. The Mogul armies were seriously handicapped by the emperor's distrust of all his principal officers, which led him into the unfortunate practice of having two or more generals, none of them definitely in supreme command, and all on the watch and suspicious of each other. From want of co-operation between the imperial forces Sivaji was enabled for the first time to inflict a severe defeat on them in the open field (1672): with the usual result for them of ill success, in the removal of the commanders and the appearance of a new viceroy for the Dekhan. The need however for military measures in other parts of the Empire made it necessary to suspend active operations against the Marathas for a time.

The institution known as *chauth* or *chout* dates from this last incursion of Sivaji into Mogul territory. He demanded one-fourth of the revenue of the invaded provinces as blackmail in the sense in which that term was applied by the reivers of the Scottish Highlands—a payment in consideration of which the contributing districts were to be guaranteed by the blackmailer against further spoliation. **Chauth.**

The suspension of hostilities by the Mogul government left Sivaji free to extend his conquests southward and eastwards over Bijapur territory, the death of the Bijapur king having left a young child on the throne. His pose as a hero of Hinduism, and his further assumption of regal dignities and splendours, set the imperial forces in motion against him once more: but only to bring about vigorous retaliatory incursions into Berar and even Gujerat. Sivaji then turned his attention once more to the south, and making an alliance with the King of Golconda who undertook to cover his rear against possible attacks from Bijapur or on the part of the Mogul, he set about the subjugation of the greater part of Mysore and the Carnatic; occupying part of the conquered territory and leaving part in possession of the previous proprietor on condition of receiving half the revenue. This applied to the tract which had been held as a jaghir by his father Shahji. The aggression of the Moguls in the meantime enabled him to carry his plans to formal completeness; their attack on Bijapur causing the regency there to call for Sivaji's assistance, as the price of which he demanded the entire cession of Sivaji's jaghir, and of other territory in addition. **Sivaji extends his dominions southwards.**

But death prevented him from making his dominions secure. He fell ill and died early in 1680. Though the son of a great magnate, he had practically started his own career as a brigand chief. By treachery, cajolery, and sheer **Death of Sivaji.**

hard fighting he had when he died at the age of fifty-three made himself and his Marathas masters of the Konkans—the coast and mountain strip running from Goa up to Kandesh—and of half Mysore and the Carnatic; laying very substantially the foundations of the great Maratha Dominion. He was succeeded by his Son Sambăji, a dissolute and violent prince who had already once deserted to the Moguls; a succession with the usual accompaniments of a rival nominee, much bloodshed, and serious if temporary disintegration of the Maratha power.

Aurangzib policy in the Dekhan.

In 1683 Aurangzib had made terms with the Raja of Udaipur; Sambaji was acknowledged head of the Marathas and had just been joined by the Mogul prince Akbar. With a curious lack of perception Aurangzib, who had resolved to make himself master of the Dekhan, decided to destroy the monarchies of Bijapur and Golconda before curbing the Marathas—perhaps imagining that the last named would no longer prove really formidable now that Sivaji was dead. He also found this a fitting opportunity for pressing the enforcement of the revived poll-tax on Hindus, thereby exciting the animosity of the great bulk of the Dekhan population. Finally, he adopted a plan of campaign unsuited to the country in which he had to work; and vitiated by that distrust of any and every general which led him to combine incompatibles in one command, and to allow no one a sufficient body of troops for the particular ends that he was ordered to achieve. Consequently one prince marched through the Konkans (where the Marathas evaded battle), losing men and killing horses in large numbers by the way; and another prince moved on Bijapur from the north-east. When these two armies had got well to the south, Sambaji emerged, and raided into Gujerat and Berar: the princes in the meantime finding themselves in insufficient force to attack Bijapur with effect.

End of the Dekhan kingdoms.

Finding that Sambaji was now in alliance with Golconda, Aurangzib turned on the latter kingdom, where the rivalry of the Mussulman commander and the Brahmin chief minister resulted in the desertion of the former with most of the army—which, as always in the Mohammedan kingdoms, consisted largely of Pathans or Afghans: the capital, Haidarabad, was sacked, and a heavy money payment exacted from the king. Reverting to Bijapur, where the resistance seems somewhat unaccountably to have melted away, he captured it very shortly after completing the investment, and then once more fell upon Golconda; abolishing the two monarchies, absorbing them into provinces of the Empire, and establishing a military occupation as far south as Tanjur. These successes were rounded off by the unexpected capture of the person of Sambaji, and his execution; followed not long after by the capture of Raighar, and with it Saho the infant son and recognised heir of Sambaji.

Maratha resistance.

Now ensued a long guerilla war. Raja Rām, uncle of Saho, acting as regent in his name, escaped from the Konkans where large Mogul forces were in comparatively dangerous proximity, to the strong fort of Jinji or Gingee in the Carnatic; while all over the Maratha country the chiefs were instructed and encouraged to carry into the Mogul territories an organised and lucrative system of raiding and plundering. The next few years passed in a process of the gradual reduction of Maratha forts by the emperor, and the constant retaliatory raids of the Marathas: a process under which on the whole the Marathas seemed to thrive, not only carrying their incursions into Malwa, but presently attaining such strength as to set about recapturing the captured forts: while a constantly increasing demoralisation was sapping the effectiveness of the Mogul armies.

Death of Aurangzib

At last, in 1707, in the forty-ninth year of his rule, and the eighty-ninth of his life, the last great ruler of the Mogul family died. A grim and austere zealot, with an immense capacity for work, a remarkable grasp of detail, and insatiable ambition, he extended the bounds of his empire far beyond the limits of his ancestral dominion; but in such wise that it straightway fell to pieces in fact if not in form as soon as the reins dropped from his hands; and even in the hour of his death the coming doom of the Empire was foreseen by shrewd observers.

Aurangzib's successors.

After Aurangzib's death, definite policy disappears from the counsels of his successors. His son Moazzim, who had seen much service and acquitted himself with credit in the Dekhan, became emperor under the title of Bahādur Shah, being already over sixty years old. The five years of his reign were mainly occupied in maintaining the throne against his brothers and in composing complications in Rajputana. Incidentally, Saho the grandson of Sivaji was set at liberty, and Maratha activities were in some degree absorbed by internal dissensions in consequence; the son of the late regent having been set up as a rival claimant to the succession. Bahadur Shah was succeeded by his son Jehāndar Shah, who in his turn was deposed and executed by a nephew, Farokshīr, a year later, the control of the government falling into the hands of the Seiads, Abdallah Khan and Hosein Ali, of Mohammed's line. (1713.)

Rise of the Peshwas.

Thenceforth, the empire became a mere hot-bed of intrigues, open revolts, and gradual assertion by viceroys of *de facto* (though not *de jure*) independence; the fruits of these troubles being appropriated mainly by the Marathas. Among them, two families first rise into prominence—that of the Brahmin Bālaji Wiswanath, from whom sprang the Pēshwas who gradually obtained recognition as the real heads of the Maratha confederacy: and that of Pantoji Bhonsla, who, though apparently not connected with the family of Sivaji, for a long time contested the supremacy of the Peshwas—each appearing in the character of a hereditary minister of the nominal monarch, Sivaji's descendant. The marked ability not only of Balaji Wiswanath, but still more of his son Bāji Rao and his grandson Balaji Rao ultimately secured the Peshwa predominance; three other families—the Gaikwars of Baroda, the Sindhias, and the Holkars—also acquiring prominence, but none of them for many years aspiring to the actual supremacy of the Maratha confederacy; while the Peshwas themselves continued to recognise the nominal authority of Sivaji's successors.

Break up of the Mogul Empire.

The immense extension of the Maratha power over the vast dominion shewn in the Map (II) really took place roughly between 1720 and 1750; the imperial province of the Dekhan, with the Carnatic under a subordinate governor or Nawāb being consolidated during much the same period into a powerful independent state by the Nizam-ūl-Mūlk, Asaf Jah. The death-blow to the real Mogul Power was dealt by the great invasion of Nadir Shah from Persia, and the sack of Delhi in 1739.

The administration of the Seiads (1713-1720), which terminated shortly after the accession of Mohammed Shah to the throne of the Moguls, is notable chiefly for the treaty made with Saho by Hosein Ali—whereby the Maratha was officially confirmed in authority over all the districts possessed by Sivaji as well as subsequent conquests, and also in his claim to the *chauth* (one fourth of the revenue) of the Dekhan, and ten per cent. of the remaining revenue; in return for which he was to guarantee the whole district against any depredations, to furnish 15,000 horse, and to pay a tribute of about £100,000 recognising what may be called the Suzerainty of the Emperor. This treaty was repudiated at the time by Farokshir, but was confirmed afterwards by Mohammed Shah.

For a brief period after the fall of the Seiads, Asaf Jah, already viceroy of the Dekhan, acted as Wazir. It was not long however before he became disgusted with the court, and withdrew to his province, in which from thenceforth he made the merest pretence of submission to the Imperial authority, at the same time encouraging the aggressive advance of the Marathas in Hindostan in order to divert them from hostilities in the Dekhan itself. Haidarabad now becomes the capital of the Nizam's dominions. The Carnatic remained under the governorship of the family to which it had been delegated about 1710 by a predecessor of the Nizam. Asaf Jah, the Nizam-ul-Mulk.

Between 1720 and 1730, then, the great divisions and dynasties with whom the British were shortly to come into conflict have approximately taken form. The grandson of Sivaji is at the head of the Maratha nation; Balaji Wiswanath the Peshwa, (succeeded by his son Baji Rao), and the Bhonsla, are the two chief ministers whose offices are to become hereditary; Sindhia, Holkar, and the Gaikwar, are taking their places as the leading chiefs, though they have not yet absorbed the tracts of Hindostan The new Powers.

which are to be acquired by them in the next few years. The Nizam has virtually declared the independence of the Dekhan. Rajputana is practically an independent confederacy. Sādat Khan, founder of the family of the Oudh kings is coming to the front in that province; Ali Vardi Khan, grandfather of the notorious Surāj-ud-Daulah (of the Black Hole) is about to acquire a similar ascendancy in Bengal.

Between 1730 and 1740 Baji Rao practically obtained from the Mogul the cession of Malwa, of Gujerat, and of Bandelkhand (Bundelcund). But his progress was temporarily checked by the unexpected and devastating invasion of Nadir Shah.

Nadir Shah. Since the arrival of the Moguls in Hindostan there had been no great invasion through the Afghan passes. It was a Persian invader who at length shattered the Mogul power, leaving the emperor practically at the mercy of his viceroys and of the Marathas. About 1720 the Safavi or "Sofy" dynasty of Persia was dispossessed by the Afghan tribe of Ghilzais, whose chief, Mahmud, made himself Shah. But a great Persian warrior arose, Nadir Kuli, who in turn drove out the Ghilzais; and after waging successful war against the aggression of the Western Turks, during which time figureheads of the Safavi family occupied the throne, was himself elected to the crown as Nadir Shah, in 1736. The annexation of Afghanistan as far as Kandahar—the Ghilzai country—brought Nadir Shah's borders in contact with those of the Mogul empire, which still embraced Ghazni (Guznee) and Kabul. Nadir Shah regarded the conduct of the Delhi court in connection with a diplomatic incident, as an adequate *casus belli.* Kabul was promptly taken: while the Mogul court, regarding the danger from Afghanistan as distant, and that from the Marathas as urgent, paid little attention to what was going on beyond the Indus. But the hill tribes did not offer the expected resistance to the invader; the Sikhs, who later on became a formidable barrier, had recently been almost crushed out of existence; and Nadir Shah was very soon across the Satlej. The Mogul army was routed with ease, and the Mogul himself had to visit Nadir's camp and tender submission. (March 1739.) The two monarchs, on apparently friendly terms, proceeded to Delhi accompanied by Nadir's army. The mob rose against the invaders; and after many had been killed, Nadir, who at first had attempted to restrain the disturbance, lost his self-control, and ordered a general massacre, which was not stayed till the slaughter had continued with every accompaniment of uncurbed ferocity for the greater part of a day. The city was then systematically and thoroughly sacked; the inhabitants were compelled under torture to disclose their treasures; persons of position were held to ransom. It was not till the country had been sucked dry of treasure like a squeezed sponge that Nadir Shah restored the crown to Mohammed Shah and withdrew; having had the trans-Indus dominions of the Moguls ceded to him, in addition to the untold booty he was carrying off.

The sack of Delhi.

These events bring us down to the time when the Frenchman Dupleix, in the Carnatic began to lay his plans for that aggressive policy which forced French and British alike into the arena of native politics. For nearly a decade, however, the complications with the European Companies were confined to the Carnatic, and acquired no importance in the eyes of the native rulers; and this chapter may appropriately conclude with a summary of the Maratha extension during that period.

Extension of Maratha dominion.

The Peshwa had been completely taken aback by Nadir's invasion, and his first thought was that Hindostan must unite against the common enemy. But when the Persian monarch retired, and seemed to have no intention of returning, matters assumed a different aspect. The Bhonsla, now established at Nagpur in Berar, extended his predatory incursions southward into the heart of the Carnatic and northward up to the Ganges. Balaji Rao, who succeeded his father as Peshwa in 1740, at first supported the Moguls, getting his own claims on Malwa confirmed: but he then made terms with the Nagpur Raja, with the result that the latter obtained further cession of territory as far as Kattak (Cuttack) in Orissa, and received chauth from the Nawab of

Bengal. Malwa was apportioned to Holkar and Sindhia, and Gujerat to the Gaikwar; so that the Maratha domain now reached from sea to sea between the Ganges basin on the north and the Nizam's dominions on the south.

Finally the death of the Raja Saho without issue in 1749 was followed next year by the recognition of the Peshwa as head of the whole Maratha confederacy, at Puna; with a *roi fainéant* lacking even the shadow of authority, in the person of a supposed grandson of Raja Ram (the regent when Sambaji died) to represent the house of Sivaji.

CHAPTER IV

THE EUROPEAN TRADERS

(*Maps I and II*)

UNTIL the close of the fifteenth century, India was an almost mythical country to the nations of the west. Alexander had entered the Panjab, and after him occasional Greeks penetrated into Hindostan; but it lay beyond the borders of the Roman empire, beyond the range of maritime adventure. The sailors of Venice and Genoa were limited virtually to the Mediterranean, and the commerce of India found its way to European markets mainly through the Levant. But the great Oceanic movement of the fifteenth century brought about the discovery of America by Columbus and of the Cape Route to India, first sailed by Vasco di Gama in 1497. The great commerce passed from the Italian States to the countries with an Atlantic sea-board, Spain and Portugal leading till their supremacy was challenged by England and Holland and finally by France.

The Indian Myth.

Discovery of the Cape Route.

The great discoveries led to a remarkable Papal pronouncement, by which the new world was parted between Spain and Portugal. The new century was more than half over before English sailors began to make a claim in America on their own account: and the Portuguese had been established on the coast of India, and in the Spice Islands, for a full hundred years before the English and the Dutch commenced active trading operations in those regions. The Portuguese, then, were the pioneers. Their energy in the early part of the sixteenth century was immense; and in the first quarter of it, Albuquerque had already established a maritime empire in the Indian Ocean. The Mogul dominion was not yet created: the Maratha name

The Portuguese.

was unknown. The Portuguese ruled the sea, but made no attempt to usurp sovereignty by land. Their principal settlement at Goa on the Malabar coast was practically impregnable. In India, they had not to deal with a folk so unsophisticated in the arts of war as were found by the Spaniards in Mexico and Peru; the Indian artillery was good and plentiful; still the lesson was early learned of the difference between European and Oriental discipline, and it was quickly found that a handful of resolute adventurers could defy a host of native levies. On the other hand it was soon apparent that while the presence of Portuguese fleets offered no menace to the Country Powers, the trade they brought was extremely desirable. Yet the kings of Gujerat and the Dekhan coast varied between fear and favour towards the foreigners; and twice at least great combined attempts were made to annihilate them, about the middle of the century and again in 1570. The attempts were met and frustrated with stubborn valour, and the Portuguese fleets remained supreme.

But in 1580 the absorption of Portugal by Spain robbed the smaller country of life and energy. A few years later, the independence of Holland had become an established fact and the naval supremacy had passed from Spain to the land of Drake and Hawkins. In India the Empire of Hindostan had again taken enduring form under Akbar. English merchants began to dream of wealth to be gathered in the East as well as in the West. A merchant adventurer named Fitch, carrying letters from Elizabeth herself, made a tour of enquiry in India, bringing home golden reports. In 1599, an association was formed in London for Eastern trade which was incorporated by Charter in the following year, with exclusive rights. The East India Company was born. Dutch ships had already rounded the Cape; in 1603 the Dutch East India Company was established.

The British and Dutch East India Companies.

Within Asiatic waters, these companies behaved practically as if they were sovereign Powers, their proceedings having very little connection with the diplomatic relations between their governments at home. In effect, they were given exclusive rights as against other traders and were then left to take care of themselves. If they thought fit to raid each other's factories (as trading stations were called) and to sink each other's ships, no one except the injured Company objected unless in very flagrant cases: and the injured Company retaliated when opportunity offered.

The Portuguese, with military establishments at Aden and Ormuz on the Persian Gulf, at Surat and Goa, at Masulipatam and Hugli, dominated the Indian littoral. They claimed an exclusive right to the entire trade both there and in the Spice Islands. During forty years, the Dutch gradually superseded them in the Islands, and it was in the Islands also that the English Company began its operations; which when successful were extremely profitable. But within a very few years, it turned its attention to India: the Portuguese were defeated in attempting to suppress an expedition to Surat; the Mogul Jehangir was favourably disposed to competition against the Portuguese: and in 1613, an Imperial *firman* authorised the establishment of British factories at Surat and some other places.

Establishment of British factories.

The next important step was the famous embassy of Sir Thomas Roe from James I. of England and VI. of Scotland to the Court of Jehangir. Sir Thomas was much impressed by the splendour of the Court and the venality of the courtiers. He did not like the Prince who afterwards became Shah Jehan, and his admiration for Jehangir was qualified. But he obtained concessions.

Sir T. Roe's embassy.

In 1632, the Portuguese having taken an aggressive attitude in Bengal their power was destroyed by Shah Jehan. The English were then allowed to establish a factory on the Ganges Delta, but under close restrictions; the memory of the Portuguese being fresh. Shortly after, however, the good offices of a European surgeon being requisitioned for a daughter of the Emperor, Mr Boughton performed his task so successfully that he was invited to choose his own reward; and he chose nothing for himself, but much for the Company—the right of trading duty-free in Bengal, and of establishing factories. The request was granted; Boughton went to Bengal to make the arrangements; while there he was again called in professionally, by the Prince

Concessions to the British in Bengal.

who was Governor of the province; and his success was again rewarded by a permission to the Company to establish a factory at Hugli. In 1639, by the invitation of the Hindu Raja, another factory was established on the Coromandel coast, and fortified under the title of Fort St George; the city which grew up around it developing into Madras.

and on the Coromandel Coast.

The civil wars in England delayed active progress. Portugal had now fallen out of the contest, and the rivalry in Asiatic waters was between English and Dutch. The advantage lay on the side of the latter, their Company being intimately associated with the States Government, while the English were dependent on private energy and enterprise, which were handicapped by the civil broils. The Protector dealt vigorously with the Dutch, and the position was a good deal improved under his rule; but these circumstances were to a great extent responsible for the comparatively large share which India occupied of the British Company's attention, as against the Islands.

About the year 1660 three important events took place—the accession of Aurangzib in India; the restoration of Charles II. in England; and the death of Cardinal Mazarin in France. There Louis XIV. himself assumed the direction of the State, and Colbert became his chief minister. For some years to come, the political relations of England, France and Holland shifted perpetually, the European interests of England and Holland agreeing, while their commercial interests were in constant antagonism. Moreover, Colbert resolved that France should enter on the Oceanic rivalry; French fleets and harbours had unexampled sums spent on them, and the French Government gave financial support to Colonial enterprise. Under Colbert's auspices a French East India Company was formed in 1664, which after various vicissitudes finally formed its Indian headquarters at Pondichery under the remarkably able control and guidance of François Martin.

Development of French Colonial policy by Colbert.

One early consequence of the Restoration in England was the cession of Bombay to the English Crown by Portugal, under the Royal Marriage Treaty. The Crown, not seeing its way to making the most of the gift, transferred it a few years later to the East India Company; and it shortly became the principal British settlement on the West Coast.

Temporary alliance with England against Holland enabled the French Company to make a footing good in India; the flight of James II., and the accession of his son-in-law "Dutch William" in England then definitely united the Dutch and the British against the aggressive policy of Louis; and from this time, as far as India is concerned, Dutch hostility ceases to be an active factor in the Company's calculations. But a consciousness of the coming disintegration of the Empire grows. As early as 1685, the British had been audacious enough to levy war against the Mogul on account of grievances, and were in danger of being wiped out of the country, when they were saved practically owing to the Moslem fanaticism of Aurangzib. The capture of pilgrim-ships on the way to Mecca pointed to a danger which he was not prepared to face. This together with a general sense of the financial advantage derivable from the Company's trade, induced the Mogul to come to terms, and allow a fresh settlement in Bengal. The factories having been destroyed, a new settlement was made on the banks of the Hugli, which developed into Calcutta. Five years later, under the pressure of a revolt in Orissa, permission was given to erect the fortifications which became known as Fort William.

Complicated relations between France, Holland and England.

Calcutta.

The Company's monopoly of trade had long been a source of antagonism to them on the part of other merchants. In the abstract, the argument of the free-traders was sound; in the concrete, it was vitiated by conditions which the economic thesis left out of count. Trade with India was only possible if the traders were protected by land and sea. International Law gave practically no protection, and Government was not prepared to provide it. The traders therefore must be in a position to protect themselves. This the Company was able to do; interlopers, as the unlicensed traders were called, were not. Moreover the Company could control their own servants on land, and their own ships by sea; but they were held responsible by the Native authorities for the conduct of all traders of their own nation; and

The Interlopers.

this gave them a fair title to demand that none should be recognised who were not under their control. A Parliamentary Resolution affirming the right of free trading, hampered the Company, and increased the activity of interlopers; many of whom in effect became mere pirates, while the Company's servants were held liable for their misdeeds.

Cromwell in his day, had been much tempted by the offer of an association which desired to set up as rivals of the old Company; but he had not yielded. Now at the close of the century, another attempt of the same kind was made, and for a time succeeded. A new Company was formed, which offered an immense price for a charter; the existing Company could not make an adequate competitive offer; the new Company was incorporated, and the result was temporary chaos. The Native functionaries pocketed huge donations from both parties; the competition between them raised prices; while each was alternately charged with the responsibility for the exploits of the notorious pirate, Captain Kidd. Happily, both were quick to recognise that alliance was better than rivalry; and in 1702 the two Companies were amalgamated. Once more a single Company was supreme, with a Charter giving the right to make war and to conclude peace with any non-Christian Power in the East; having jurisdiction over British subjects, and authority to suppress interlopers.

A rival East India Company.

Amalgamation of the Companies.

During the earlier portion of the century, the Company is principally occupied in trying to obtain concessions from Viceroys or from the Mogul, and complaining bitterly of the price which had to be paid for them. The most important of these was granted in 1715 by a *firman* of the Mogul Farokshir, who was cured of an alarming disease by Dr Hamilton; the reward asked and obtained, as in the previous case of Boughton, being privileges for the Company in Bengal. The transaction incidentally gives a curious illustration of a powerful Viceroy's evasion of the Imperial decree. The British were given permission to purchase the *zemindari* or lordship of a number of towns in the Calcutta district, but the Viceroy forbade the zemindars to sell.

During this period, the Dutch fell more and more into the background. As Portugal had failed to maintain strength sufficient to meet the strain of a great Oceanic Empire, so Holland also became exhausted by the perpetual struggle in Europe, first with Spain, then with France, enhanced by the destructive naval conflicts with England, and sank to the position of a Power of the second rank; while in India the French under a series of able organisers and administrators took the place of the Dutch as the leading competitor with Great Britain. Retrogression of the Dutch.

The earliest efforts of the French were devoted to the establishment of a station not in the Indies but on the route thither. Before Colbert's time, they had tried to secure a position in Madagascar, which for some while continued to be the headquarters of their Eastern trade. There however, the situation was always precarious, owing to the climate, the animosity of the natives, and the difficulty offered for military movements by the nature of the country. Early in the eighteenth century, the station was transferred to the neighbouring Isles of France and Bourbon, otherwise known as the Mauritius; from whence La Bourdonnais in 1746 and Suffren in 1782 conducted the operations which for the time threatened to win for the French the superior position in Eastern waters. The French Company.

In India itself, Colbert's Company was first allowed to open a factory at Surat; and a little later, when the English and French were in alliance against the Dutch, they made good a footing on the Coromandel or Carnatic coast. The kingdom of Bijapur had not yet perished, and that district still formed a part of it. François Martin, left in charge of the Carnatic settlement, made friends with the Governor. Temporary difficulties had arisen in the way of investing the specie at his disposal in merchandise, but a loan to the Native Governor, a man of honour, was safe and profitable. When circumstances made it desirable to call in the loan some years later, Martin being by that time established at Pondichery, it was found more convenient to the Governor and more advantageous to the French, that a grant of land should be made, as an equivalent. It was consistently François Martin.

Martin's policy to impress native rulers with the idea that the French were desirable and useful tenants; and so successful was he that the fortification of Pondichery in 1789, instead of being looked on with jealousy, met with their favourable approval. A serious check to the rising and prosperous community occurred when it passed for a time into the hands of the Dutch. Martin returned to France, and when there succeeded in so impressing on the authorities the importance of the place, that its restoration was one of the stipulations in the treaty of Ryswick (1697). Martin went back as Governor, and head of the whole of the French settlements in the East; and from that time Pondichery continued to flourish.

In 1688, the factory of Chandarnagar on the Hugli was opened, but it was not till Dupleix was sent there about 1730 that the Bengal trade was really developed. In the meantime, Surat had been given up altogether, with discredit, a heavy debt being left behind. The ill effects were successfully removed by Governor Lenoir of Pondichery; who, receiving unexpected supplies from France with a promise of more to follow, wisely considered the liquidation of the Surat debt as, indirectly, a better investment than the purchase of merchandise. French credit was so immensely enhanced by this transaction, that when fresh financial difficulties arose almost immediately afterwards, assistance which would otherwise certainly not have been forthcoming was freely and without hesitation rendered by the wealthy Natives. In 1725 a new fortified port was secured on the Malabar coast by the establishment of the French at Mahi, the name of which was changed to Mahé in honour of La Bourdonnais, who had it as one of his Christian names.

Lenoir.

Finally the prestige of the French in the Carnatic was raised to an unprecedented level by the cool and far-sighted courage of Lenoir's successor Dumas. He had cultivated the friendliest relations with the reigning Nawab (the lieutenant of the Nizam) and his kinsman. In 1739 the restless Bhonsla, the Maratha Raja of Nagpur, invaded the Carnatic. The Princes placed their wives and families under the protection of Dumas at Pondichery, and he

Dumas.

accepted the charge. The Marathas defeated the Nawab's armies, and ordered Dumas to surrender the families on pain of Pondichery being demolished. Dumas showed his envoy over the place, and indicated that the Bhonsla might come and take the families if he could, but that Pondichery, their city of refuge, would be held against him to the last. The attitude of defiance was tempered by a polite present of sundry bottles of "cordial waters," and the Marathas amicably retired. The Nizam was greatly impressed by the Frenchman's courage and address, and he was rewarded by Imperial honours, and the official designation of a "Commander of five thousand."

This then, about 1741, was the position of the two rival companies. The British had been in the field about twice as long as the French. They held important fortified settlements; in the Carnatic at Madras, with the subsidiary fort of St David some hundred miles to the south: on the Hugli at Calcutta or Fort William: on the west coast at Bombay: besides minor factories, as at Surat and Patna. The French, besides minor factories, had Pondichery in the Carnatic, Chandarnagar on the Hugli, and Mahé on the west coast. The Dutch and Portuguese also had their establishments at Goa, Chinsura, Negapatam, and elsewhere: but they took no effective part in the struggle. *The rival National Companies.*

Essentially, the conditions were nearly the same for both. Governors in India could follow their own line, without waiting for the endorsement of Directors at home: but if the Directors ultimately refused endorsement, the Indian Governor was liable to complete shipwreck. What Directors at home wanted was dividends; they could be relied on to estimate Glory in pounds, shillings and pence. But there was an important difference in their several relations to the National Government at home. The French Company was a perpetual tax on the Exchequer: the English Company paid money into it. Consequently there was a standing inducement to the British Government to support the Company even at some risk. In France the inducement was to be deaf to the Company's appeals. Consequently, though the Indian Governors of both might be equally *Relations of the Companies to their Governments.*

enterprising, the attitude at home was more antagonistic to enterprise in France than in England. If by any accident the will to back the respective Companies should become equalised, the present strength of the two in India was fairly equal, but the French had the advantage of the special prestige acquired by Dumas with the Natives: so that a contest would turn on the comparative ability of the home-governments to throw their weight into the scale. As it was however, the favourable inclination of the British Government was the stronger, and events proved its naval preponderance to be so complete as entirely to cancel any advantage won by the temporary superiority of the French *personnel* upon Indian soil.

Constitution of the British Company in India.

Finally we may observe the Constitution of the British Company, as bearing upon the problems developed when it became an actual territorial Power. In India itself, the Company's possessions were divided between three independent Presidencies, in Bengal, Madras and Bombay. Each Presidency had its own Governor and Council, with its servants graded as senior and junior Merchants, and Writers. The salaries of all were so low that they were in effect allowed to increase their incomes by unrestricted private trading. The governing bodies had jurisdiction within their own areas; but whatever lands they held, they held as tenants of the Country Powers. They had authority to raise troops, of which they maintained only a few hundreds until the practice of raising and training regiments of Sepoys was developed; and their chief settlements were fortified; but none of the Carnatic ports had adequate harbourage for shelter when the monsoons set in.

Home constitution of the E.I.C.

The power however of the authorities in India was modified by that of the superior authorities at home. When twelve months was about the least time that could pass between the sending of a dispatch and the receipt of the answer thereto, it was obvious that very much must be left to the judgment of the authority on the spot. Yet it was necessary to avoid steps which would involve a grave risk of censure, and no line of policy could be adopted which would seriously subvert that laid down in instructions from home. Finally, it was possible for collisions to occur between the two governing bodies in London—the Court of Proprietors, consisting of all who held five hundred pounds worth of stock, to whom lay the final appeal, and the Court of Directors, elected from the Proprietors. in whose hands was the general management; to which possibility may be added that of Parliamentary pressure, whenever questions could be raised as to the scope of the Company's Charter, and the legitimacy of introducing modification therein.

CHAPTER V

RULERS AND SUBJECTS

THE direct contest between French and British in India began in the fifth decade of the eighteenth century. A hundred years before, all Hindostan—from the Indus to the Brahmaputra, from the Himalayas to the Nerbadda—had for some time acknowledged one sovereign. South of the Nerbadda, though the great kingdom of Ahmednagar was in its last throes, Bijapur and Golconda still maintained independence. Between 1640 and 1700, for the most part in the long reign of Aurangzib, all three bowed to the yoke of the Mogul: but during the same period, Sivaji made his Marathas *de facto* lords over great part of the Dekhan.

Distribution of the Indian Powers.

At the end of the next forty years, the Mogul was reigning at Delhi by permission of Nadir Shah the Persian: the governor of Oudh called himself the Mogul's Wazir, but was independent; the governor of Bengal and Behar was equally independent: the Marathas had extended their rule over so much of Hindostan as lay between the Chambal, the Jamna, and the Nerbadda; as well as over parts of the Dekhan. Over the rest of the Dekhan the Nizam held sway, with the barest pretence of acknowledging the overlordship of Delhi, and having delegated his authority over the Carnatic to a loyal Nawab of his own choosing. The Panjab was a hunting ground for Afghan invaders: Rajputana, a collection of principalities where no strong hand ruled, and the chiefs had long unlearnt any but the most primitive arts of government. And upon the sea coast, or on a great estuary, here and there was a petty colony of European traders, French or British or Dutch; owning two or three forts and a few companies of drilled white men.

During the last century there was no respect in which India had progressed. In the Dekhan the rule of the Mogul governors was no whit better than that of the royal lines of Bijapur and Golconda. The Marathas were as rapacious as the Mussulman Lords, more blood-thirsty and restless, even less vexed with theories about the good of the governed. The Provincial Governors of the Empire were concerned in establishing their own power and independence. Before the disintegration set in, Aurangzib had deserted the comparatively liberal policy of his predecessors. In those years, every reproach that could be urged against the Mogul government became intensified; and history gives no sign that there was anywhere existing either the will or the capacity to reorganise order out of the growing chaos. Character of the Government since Aurangzib.

Immense progress had been made under the wise sway of Akbar; but it had been his task to introduce order and system where they had never yet prevailed, at the same time that he was establishing a new dynasty. No great positive prosperity could therefore be reached. The way was made ready by him for his son and grandson, and it is only natural that, by common consent, the most prosperous period of Hindostan was in the reign of Shah Jehan. When Aurangzib seated himself upon his father's throne, there arrived at the court of the old Mogul a French Physician, François Bernier, who left to posterity sundry vivid descriptions of men, manners, and events in India as he saw them with keen observant eyes and an honest, intelligent brain. From him we may learn what the Mogul Empire was capable of at its normal best—that is, when not under the control of that rare creation, a despot who was at once an idealist and a practical man—the best that could be provided except by an Akbar succeeding an Akbar; the best that could be maintained even for a short time, under any system of Oriental despotism. François Bernier.

The earliest records of Greeks and Romans assume the conception or idea of a State, a Body Politic; a systematic relation between the grades of society; a unity pervading each particular society and distinguishing it from others. This conception permeates all the peoples of Europe. If European conception of a State.

one State conquers another, the citizens of the conquered State sooner or later become citizens of the conquering one. The ruling and privileged classes always recognise that the State as a whole has claims upon their individual services, and that they have some sort of obligations towards the classes below them. The normal condition of affairs is an organised government which recognises and enforces in a general way the right to protection of life and property, and it is the business of the sovereign power to ensure these things in some degree. There are in every State intervals of anarchy, when every man lives by the strength of his own arm and the wiliness of his own brain; but these intervals are abnormal. Hence there is a general encouragement to industry: the private citizen can count, at least up to a certain point, on enjoying the fruits of his labours, and profiting by his accumulations and thrift. The theory is that the State is organised for the common benefit of all its constituent members, though some may claim a larger share than others in that benefit.

No such conception in India.

In India, however, this idea of the State was practically non-existent. The object of Government was to extract from the country the largest amount of revenue for the governing members; and to maintain at disposal a mass of troops which could prevent rebellion, and extend dominion.

The Oriental System.

Every monarch was constantly occupied either in making war on his neighbours, to exact tribute or capture their thrones, or in defending his own throne against foreign aggressors or rebels within the borders. The Empire was parcelled out into Provinces of whose rulers two things were expected—that they would march troops in the Mogul's service, and that they would produce funds for the Mogul's treasury. The Provinces were sub-divided into districts whose rulers owed a like responsibility to the Provincial Governors. Rules and regulations of procedure were laid down, on which was based the calculation of the amount which was required to be produced; but so long as that amount was forthcoming, the man at the top cared very little how far his subordinates kept to the rules in producing it. The district officer saw that the local magnate provided as much as the assessment required, and as much more as he could see his way to extract. The local magnate exacted of course from the populace as much as would satisfy the district officer: but there was practically no check on additional extortions; since there was no real means of appeal to a higher power, no court before which misrule could be challenged. Industry became absurd, when the possession of savings in any form was simply an incitement to extortion; justice was a mere travesty when its appointed administrators gave their awards in accordance with the size of the *douceurs* offered by the respective litigants. Defective Justice.

Good governors were of course to be found as well as bad, and the good governor would at any rate seek to appoint subordinates of comparatively high character; but the system offered no security. A vigorous expression of public opinion and a high individual sense of public spirit might at times and in places counteract the strong temptations to venality and indifference; but public spirit was rare and public opinion was voiceless.

In Europe, public spirit is engendered by ideas of family honour and by service traditions. Absence of Public Spirit.

In the one case a certain standard is maintained because by falling utterly below it a man loses social caste: in the other, it is maintained by *esprit de corps*. But India was the land of adventurers. Power was the reward of the daring swordsman or the crafty intriguer, whose antecedents were no bar to success. Many a governor had commenced his career as a slave. Such men had no traditions to live up to. They fought for their own hand, and when they acquired power, used it for their own immediate gratification, knowing the uncertainty of the tenure under which they held it.

The keynote of the whole system is Instability. In Europe, every reigning dynasty ruled in virtue of descent more or less direct from ancient princes: the Moguls in India dated no further back than the reign of our Henry VIII. The individual monarch secured himself on the throne usually at the cost of a war with one or another of his brothers, and possibly with his own father. He held it with a consciousness that as soon as his sons were grown Instability of Government.

up, he might have to fight them for it in turn. He lived of necessity in an atmosphere of suspicion. Jehangir intrigued against Akbar, Shah Jehan was in arms against Jehangir, Aurangzib deposed Shah Jehan; and his own latter days were a burden to him by reason of his perpetual suspicions of his own sons. Yet the circumstances, from the accession of Akbar to the death of Aurangzib a hundred and fifty years later, were extraordinarily favourable; inasmuch as there were but four reigns covering the whole period; and it might generally be said that the longer a monarch occupied the throne the firmer grew his seat.

Position of the Mohammedan Nobility. Still more uncertain was the position of the Omrahs, the Mussulman lords and officers. Their functions were not hereditary, but terminable simply at the royal pleasure. Their possessions were granted as from the Mogul, and might be renewed by him at will. It was only when the Empire was already breaking up that they began to found families. After the Mogul family, there was no Mussulman house of front rank in India whose rise was not subsequent to the death of Aurangzib, except that of Haidarabad: founded by the Nizam-ul-Mulk, himself a distinguished officer of Aurangzib, who established his family because he outlived his master by forty years. Had he died twenty or even ten years earlier, the Dekhan would have passed into other hands. In short, before the eighteenth century no Mussulman *House* could be said to exist. Akbar in his boyhood had a great minister, Bairam; and Bairam's son became one of his greatest generals; but even that was exceptional.

Insecurity of property. Hereditary position did indeed belong to the Rajput chiefs, who traced their genealogies to remote antiquity. There were even Mussulman princes as at Bhopal, whose dynasties were continuous; but in almost all cases, their power was local, limited, and maintained because it was so. The Rajas of Jodpur and Jeipur and Udaipur were usually prominent men, sometimes trusted officers of the Empire; but their dominions were all in the comparatively barren regions of Rajputana. Briefly, heredity in the possession of property applied with effect only to small estates, and did not serve as a protection against open appropriation or practical confiscation by higher powers, though it gave the chief or the village community a degree of protection as against neighbours of the same status: while the accumulation of personal wealth in the form of portable property merely provided a magnet attracting the greed of officials, who had achieved their own position mainly by making it worth the while of their superiors to appoint them.

Semblance and reality.

Under such conditions no very high pitch of prosperity could well be attained. Wealth could only accumulate in the hands of the few nobles who had strength and wit to keep it by force. The Court was magnificent, beyond European parallel; but there the splendour ended. There were glorious buildings at Delhi and Agra; but apart from mosques and palaces, these cities were constructed more as if intended to be temporary camps than anything else. The Moguls raised monumental structures, they made some great roads and canals. But this had more to do with making things pleasant for themselves and their *entourage*, than with thought for the public good. The works were constructed by the forced labour of the peasantry in the districts selected for Imperial residence. And it is to be remarked that wherever the Mogul was in person, there also was a large army, with innumerable camp-followers. As the great Court moved from spot to spot in its leisurely progresses, the populace was subjected to constant and heavy contributions. The emperors were in the habit of holding audiences for dispensing justice, and they enjoyed the *rôle*—which indeed they filled with credit—of "protectors of the poor" in a strictly personal capacity; but one *cadi* or magistrate could accomplish more injustice in a day than the Mogul could remedy in a week. When the ordinary channels of the law were hopelessly polluted, and no effort was made to cleanse them, the beneficent decisions in occasional cases were a very inefficient antidote. The high standard set by Akbar himself and the men he selected was not maintained even by his two immediate successors, as was testified by Sir Thomas Roe in Jehangir's time, and by Bernier in the last days of Shah Jehan. When the ruler never hesitated to make away with any inconvenient person, human life was likely to be held cheap; when he could transfer any subject's property to his own coffers without scandal, respect for the rights of others was not likely to prevail in less exalted ranks.

The soldiery. The armies of the Moguls were counted in myriads; but they were in fact made up in great part of very ill-disciplined mercenaries. Their military value was gauged—and over-rated—by Bernier, when he said that Condé or Turenne with twenty-five thousand Frenchmen could shatter the whole power of the Empire. The support of this vast number of troops, of whom an immense proportion were mounted, was a constant drain on the resources of the country; and the soldiery supplemented their legitimate maintenance by forcible exactions. Matters became worse with the development of the Maratha power, whose hordes of light horsemen swept the country, stuffing their saddle-bags as they went, and claiming *chauth* from the rulers in addition to their other spoils. They surged northward up to the gates of Delhi and southward into the Carnatic: in self-defence, Calcutta had to construct the famous "Maratha ditch"; where they passed, rapine and pillage accompanied them. And finally, where there were hills, there were fortresses, and where there were fortresses there were robbers.

Condition of the population. Oppression and lawlessness were not indeed carried to the point at which industry perishes altogether; the same sort of protection was extended to the trading classes as was granted to Jews in Mediæval Europe; they were a convenience to their masters, as long as they could pay ransom. But enterprise has little chance under such conditions; its rewards are insufficient save in the eyes of the few; and commerce was further hampered by the imposition of innumerable taxes, market dues, and tolls. The mass of the population attempted to do little more than to live from hand to mouth, with at the most an effort to collect and bury in some secret place enough to provide the cost of marrying a daughter.

Such were the general results of Mohammedan or Maratha supremacy. There was no inducement to progress, except where a particular Governor happened to be endowed with a higher sense of duty, or a keener perception of the sources of wealth, than most of his compeers. There were such exceptions, and so one district or another, one town or another, would flourish for a season; but there is small room to doubt that in respect of the prevalent conditions of life, India at the time when the House of Hanover succeeded to the throne of Great Britain was five hundred years behind Europe: while she showed no sign of containing within herself the germs of redemption.

The European communities.

As for the little European communities, they consisted practically of exiles, many of whom never set foot again on their native shores after they had once landed in India: or, if they did so, found that the habits they had contracted in the East were not easily made compatible with Western social conditions. The extent to which they were cut off from European associations is not readily realised until we remember that a favourable voyage round the Cape rarely occupied much less than six months; and that something like a year and a half actually elapsed between the time of Clive's sailing from England, and his landing at Madras.